UG 2 9 1996

D0677724

Southern Folk, Plain & Fancy

DISCARDED
From Nashville Public Library

Property of
The Public Library of Nashville and Davidson County
225 Polk Ave., Nashville, TN 37203
SOUTHEAST BRANCH LIBRARY

John Shelton Reed

Southern Folk, Plain & Fancy

Native White Social Types

Mercer University   Lamar Memorial Lectures No. 29

The University of Georgia Press   Athens and London

© 1986 by the University of Georgia Press
Athens, Georgia 30602
All rights reserved

Designed by Sandra Strother Hudson
Set in Linotron 9 on 12 Bookman

The paper in this book meets the guidelines for
permanence and durability of the Committee on
Production Guidelines for Book Longevity of the
Council on Library Resources.

Printed in the United States of America

92 91 90 89 88   5 4 3 2

Library of Congress Cataloging in Publication Data

Reed, John Shelton.
  Southern folk, plain and fancy.

  (Lamar memorial lectures / Mercer University;
  no. 29) Lectures delivered Oct. 1985.
  Bibliography: p.
  Includes index.
  1. Southern States—Social life and customs.
2. Southern States—Popular culture.   I. Title.
II. Series: Lamar memorial lectures; no. 29.
F216.2.R435 1986   306′.0975   86-1479
ISBN 0-8203-0862-5 (alk. paper)
ISBN 0-8203-1023-9 (pbk.: alk. paper)

Contents

Foreword

We at Mercer University consider it our great good fortune to have had Professor and Mrs. John Shelton Reed as guests on our campus in October 1985, when Mr. Reed delivered the twenty-ninth annual Lamar Memorial Lectures. Despite competition from the Georgia State Fair in Macon and from the World Series on television, Professor Reed spoke to large and appreciative audiences of not only faculty and townspeople but students as well. Growing out of his lectures, *Southern Folk, Plain and Fancy,* with its impressive research in scholarly and popular sources and its lively vernacular style, is a significant addition to the study of Southern culture.

In many of his earlier writings, Professor Reed focused upon the South as a unit and upon how people perceive the region to be different from the rest of the country. As he makes clear in this volume, the uniqueness of the South's social types contributes much to such a perception. Yet if there is one South, there are also many Souths rising out of the different social types within the region itself. *Southern Folk, Plain and Fancy* classifies the fascinating specimens of those types that thrive below the Potomac: Southern ladies and gentlemen, good old boys and girls, rednecks, and others. Using Daniel R. Hundley's important but little-known *Social Relations in Our Southern States* (1860) as the touchstone for his own discussion, Professor Reed traces the genealogy of these types, most of which were well-established in antebellum days. He also assays the limitations of social types as a reflection of a society's complexity, describes their manipulation by the popular culture of our time, and suggests why they will continue to exist. All the while, he points up the utility of social types as indicators of what people think of the South and its inhabitants. Throughout, he brings to his study the skills of the social scientist, the sensibility of the humanist, a keen eye for irony, and a delightful sense of humor.

The Lamar Lectures series, which is made possible by the generosity of the late Eugenia Dorothy Blount Lamar, is admirably enhanced by Professor Reed's contribution.

Wayne Mixon
for the
Lamar Memorial Lectures Committee

Preface

Reworking for publication what was originally written as a set of lectures has made me acutely aware of the differences between the two forms. I fear that the odor of the podium still clings to my text in many places, but I cannot dispel it entirely without undertaking to write an altogether different book, which might not be a bad idea, but is pretty far down my list of things to do any time soon. So I ask readers to place themselves imaginatively in the audience for whom these remarks were originally intended: a group composed primarily of Southerners with an amateur or professional interest in their region's history and culture, gathered on Mrs. Lamar's generous foundation at Mercer University in the fall of 1985. Then, perhaps, they will excuse a rather colloquial tone, some attempts at in-group humor, and the occasional *ex cathedra* pronouncement.

Even this essay's purpose reflects its origins. Public lectures are not the place to attempt a scholarly synthesis, to pick a monographic quarrel, or even to develop a closely-reasoned argument. On the other hand, they are ideally suited for poking about, for speculating, for spinning hypotheses rather than testing them in any rigorous way. That is what I have tried to do here.

I hope my lectures reflected the available scholarship, but I did not try seriously to criticize that literature or even to summarize it, and I have not done so in this revision, either. Nor did I cite only works of certified scholarship. This essay explores a territory—that of everyday life, seemingly trivial and ephemeral—where the learned sometimes disdain to tread, and often a particular terrain had been mapped only by a "mere journalist." (I will never use that phrase again without heavy irony.) Even when the ground was well-explored scholarly turf, I sometimes chose a journalist's colorful description over one more guarded, academic, and strictly verifiable. So long as the important features of the landscape are noted, I see no real harm in this; I have dozed through too many lectures in my time to ignore the problem of boredom.

Two other peculiarities of this book can be traced to its original form. Here, as in the lectures, I have freely made direct reference to a variety of popular culture materials—not only to the surprisingly many learned articles *about* country music, for example, but to the lyrics of country music itself—without the sort of explicit methodological care that (for good reason) usually accompanies the analysis of such data. In addition, I have not hesitated (or not much) to draw on my own observations, systematic and otherwise. If an anthropologist can make a career as an expert after a year among the Bagu-bagu, why should I feel apologetic about discussing a tribe that I have been observing for forty-odd years? (Nevertheless, I do, although more in print than in lectures.)

I am resigned to this book's proving to be transitory, in many respects. Many of the references will no doubt already mystify those whose tastes in leisure-time activity differ from mine, and so many examples are drawn from popular culture and public life of the 1960s, 1970s, and 1980s that they are doomed to be dated in a decade, obscure in a generation, and unintelligible in fifty years. Perhaps I should have included textual notes in anticipation, thus: Boss Hogg.* But where would I have stopped? Jimmy Carter?† No, late twenty-first-century readers will have to fend for themselves.

But such readers, if there are any, will have a compensating advantage. They will know the answers to the list of questions with which this book concludes. I would not be surprised if the basic outlines of this analysis were still applicable. If so, perhaps they will read about the Southern types of 1985 with the same excitement and sense of recognition with

---

*Continuing character on "The Dukes of Hazzard" television program, ca. 1980. Principal characteristic: ineffectual malice.

†President of the United States, 1976–80. Principal characteristic: ineffectual good intentions.

which I read about the types of 1860 in Daniel Hundley's *Social Relations in Our Southern States*, a book I have put to a great deal of use in these pages.

That will remain for me a pleasant thought, since it is obviously not subject to short-run disconfirmation. It is only one of many pleasures associated with this undertaking, and I want to thank the many people who made it so pleasant.

Mrs. Lamar's generosity and devotion to the South, and the stewardship of the Lamar Memorial Lectures Committee, have produced such a distinguished company of Lamar Lecturers that it is a great (indeed, somewhat intimidating) honor to be asked to join their number. I am grateful to Mrs. Lamar for her benefaction, and to the committee for that invitation.

To all of the Mercer people and other Maconites who made our visit so pleasant, Dale and I extend our thanks. Professor Henry Y. Warnock, chairman of the committee when the invitation was made, was a gracious and knowledgeable guide to his city during our visit. He is that fabled but all-too-rare combination, a gentleman and a scholar. His successor as chairman, Professor Wayne Mixon, was a thoughtful and congenial host. He and his wife, Fran, reminded us once again why Southern hospitality has attained mythic dimensions. I know that he must have scurried about attending to all sorts of details, but I only know it because everything went so smoothly. Wayne may be well organized, but he's a good old boy.

In writing the lectures, I had the help of friends from many disciplines and many states who send me clippings and reprints. (You *know* what I like—and I appreciate it.) Many of these correspondents are former participants in three NEH Summer Seminars that I have directed at Chapel Hill. Those seminars encountered an embryonic form of the typology developed here, and the final version is better for their comments and criticisms.

Much of my reading was done during a year at the National Humanities Center, in intervals snatched from another project. I am grateful especially to Allen Tuttle and the Center's superb library staff, who tracked down some very *peculiar* references.

Thanks also to the University of Georgia Press. Loris Green did a tactful job of copyediting, and Malcolm Call was supportive and helpful in all respects.

A word, in addition, about the illustrations. Lynn Whitener helped me locate them, just for the fun of it, and I appreciate that very much. The holders of the rights are acknowledged *in situ*, so to speak, but I thank the many organizations and individuals who kindly let me use their material for nothing, or next to it, especially the John Edwards Memorial Collection at the University of North Carolina at Chapel Hill and the Film Stills Archive of the Museum of Modern Art. This volume would be far less interesting to look at if I had not happened upon the marvelous resources of these institutions. I also would like to acknowledge, with thanks, a small grant from the College of Arts and Sciences at Chapel Hill that helped to pay for the illustrations.

My friend and colleague, George Tindall, broke some of this ground several years back. He read my manuscript and did not suggest any changes, which I took to mean that he approved of it. Come to think of it, though, he never said so. Since he may have been just being polite, he should probably not be held accountable for how I have done this, but certainly he is largely responsible for my trying in the first place.

My wife Dale remains my best and most constructive critic. She *is* responsible, for everything.

This volume is dedicated, with love, to my brothers and sisters: Lisa, Bill, Michael, and Jane. Unity in diversity.

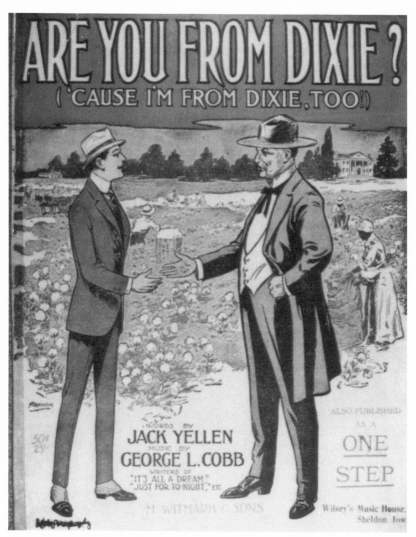

The Old South greets the New, ca. 1915. (John Edwards Memorial Collection, University of North Carolina, Chapel Hill.)

Introduction

Every human group likes to believe itself unusual, but not all aspire to be thought fascinating. Think only of Canadians, who, through a sort of cultural jiujitsu, have come to be perceived, and even to perceive themselves, as extraordinarily ordinary. Canada's tourism minister, Thomas McMillan, got it just about right when he told the *Wall Street Journal* that "We're seen as a country of great natural beauty, fresh air and fish, but not as a place to boogie."[1]

The South, of course, has been another matter. Robbie Robertson, a Canadian-born rock musician, says that "The South is the only place we play where everybody can clap on the off-beat."[2] A natural sense of rhythm: just one reason Southerners have become "a mythological people, created half out of dream and half out of slander, who live in a still legendary land." Thus spake Jonathan Daniels, and other Southerners have liked to agree with him.[3]

Faulkner juxtaposed the South and Canada by giving Quentin Compson a Canadian roommate at Harvard. Hear the Canadian's response to the hair-raising story of Colonel Thomas Sutpen: "So he just wanted a grandson. That was all he was after. Jesus, the South is fine, isn't it. . . . It's better than Ben Hur, isn't it."[4]

The psychic landscape of the South has always been peopled with strange and wonderful creatures, offering what one observer has called "a kind of running domestic theater of the dreamy and fantastic."[5] The phrase "the South" has conjured up a variety of images, but—say what you will—none of them has been ordinary, none of them banal. This strange land, the South of the mind, is where my interests as a social psychologist converge with the interests of historians and literary schol-

1

ars. What I would call regional stereotypes, historians have called regional mythology and literary scholars regional imagery.[6] I want to explore that common ground.

Although researchers like me have sometimes asked people to describe "Southerners," unqualified, we recognize, as anyone must, that there are many *kinds* of Southerners and that each summons up its own imagery, requires its own description. "Like Southern blacks," F. N. Boney writes, "Southern whites appear homogeneous only when carelessly viewed from a great distance."[7]

C. Vann Woodward made the same point in a 1972 lecture at Chapel Hill. "There [is] not one Southern style but many, and there always have been. What we need is a typology of Southern styles."[8] Woodward made it plain that he was seeking something of a field guide to the human fauna of the South, a catalog of what the sociologist Orrin Klapp has called *social types*.[9]

How do non-Southerners divide up the Southern population for discussion? How do Southerners do it? Can we develop—or rather uncover—a vernacular classification of Southern social types? We can start by examining the words that Americans use to talk about different types of Southerners: words like lady, gentleman, redneck, belle, good old boy, honkytonk angel. These and other stock characters in the Southern drama are cultural artifacts, like unicorns and trolls, elves and werewolves; they are social constructions that Southerners use to amuse each other and mystify the Yankees. But they are more than that. I will argue that these mythic inhabitants of the mythic South are approximations to real people, or, better, that they are ideals to which real people are in approximation.

Thomas Connelly has shown how Robert E. Lee became larger than life after his death.[10] Determined press-agentry had something to do with that, but it would not have worked half so well if there had not been an established type, the Southern gentleman, to which the Lee legend could be assimilated, with Lee coming to serve almost as a prototype. Similarly, now that there are songs about the hollow-eyed ghost of Hank Williams cruising Alabama in an antique Cadillac, it is obvious that he, too, has become a mythic character, a social construction. Less obviously, there is a sense in which that was true while he was still alive: the social type of the doomed victim-hero is one we shall have to examine in more detail.

First, though, we must deal with some matters of definition, warning, and ground-clearing. I will argue that regional social types are similar in form, function, and natural history to the social typology of other ethnic and national groups. For all that they play a conspicuous role in banter, humor, song, and story, social types identify real and important clusterings of characteristics and help people to make sense of the social world around them. They are primitive terms—that is, basic elements—in a sort of folk anthropology, attempts to deal with what Edgar Thompson has called the "idiomatic imponderables" of everyday life.[11] Social typing works both to smooth and to complicate interaction between different groups: we will examine that, and also the importance of the mass media in the propagation and distortion of these images.

As my title indicates, this analysis is limited to *white* Southern types. For the time being at least, black Southerners have a separate (I think far more complex and, to outsiders, far less well-known) social typology, one that could easily be the subject of another book.[12]

In Chapters 2, 3, and 4, I will array these white Southern social types, like butterflies in a case, and examine their similarities and differences. Taxonomy—cataloging—is not the most highly regarded theoretical activity in my discipline, any more than in zoology. But any culture's repertoire of social types is a good entry point for understanding what that culture approves and disapproves, what it finds amusing or pitiable, admirable or disgusting or frightening. Cataloging the South's social types, I believe, can help us to understand the South.

Taxonomy has another virtue, too. If we can sort our types by cross-tabulating a very few characteristics, we wind up with something like the periodic table of the elements, a scheme that not only orders the known, but points to other possibilities. For instance, just as there are chemical elements that are theoretical possibilities but are too unstable to be found in nature, so there are social types that, in a sense, *ought* to exist, but do not. Possibly they are "latent": perhaps they *could* come into being in the appropriate circumstances, and we can say something about what they would look like if they did. I will venture a few predictions along that line in my conclusion.

Chapter One

Social Types and How They Work

Here are some examples of social types, from Orrin Klapp's original (and now rather dated) discussion of the concept: Good joes. Old fogeys. Zoot-suiters. Sad sacks. Stuffed shirts.[1] Here are some more recent specimens: Preps. Wimps. Punks. Yuppies. Urban cowboys. Nerds. Quiche-eaters.

All of these are American social types, but they are not *regional* types. Certainly they all can be found in the South—that only goes to show that the South is part of the United States. But other social types are found nowhere else on the face of the earth. The long-haired redneck that David Allan Coe sings about, for instance, is a regional type, in a way that his distant ancestor the hippie was not.[2] There certainly are yuppies in the South, but they are everywhere these days; what other regions do *not* have is comic hillbillies (unless they are migrants from the South).

In addition, when some social type labels are prefixed with the adjective "Southern," they become something so different from the sum of their parts that they merit recognition as distinct types. Think, for instance, of the Southern gentleman, who is something more than simply a gentleman from the South. Early in this century, H. L. Mencken observed that "one searches the books in vain for mention of a . . . Yankee gentleman."[3] Sixty years later, Gail Godwin asked: "Who has ever heard of 'The Midwestern Lady,' or 'The Northern Belle'?"[4] And Florence King agreed: "There are ladies everywhere, but they enjoy generic recognition only in the South. . . . There is most assuredly a California girl, but if anyone spoke of a California lady, even Phil Donahue and Alan Alda would laugh."[5]

In the absence of evidence to the contrary, I want to assert that the

South has been America's most fecund seedbed for regional social types (although California may have been gaining on us lately), and I propose to discuss these identifiably regional characters.

But what *are* social types? I will try to answer that question, and say a few things about their natural history, how they come into being and become extinct, especially in industrial societies like our own. The mass media of communication turn out to play an important part in this. Then, I want to examine how social typing operates to structure and to complicate relations between members of different communities—for instance, between Southerners and other Americans.

Let us begin with the simple fact that there are certain noticeable clusterings of behaviors and attributes within any human population. In the South, for instance, it is not unusual to run into "a man, of any age, but more often young than not, who fits in with the status system of the region." Someone who "has a good sense of humor and enjoys ironic jokes, is tolerant and easygoing enough to get along in long conversations at places like on the corner, and has a reasonable amount of physical courage."

Most Southerners will recognize this easygoing fellow. Some will recognize where I stole the description from: It comes from Tom Wolfe's discussion of the *good old boy,* an excellent example of a regional social type.[6] Like other social types, the good old boy is a genuine social fact. Hundreds of thousands of men fill the bill, more or less. Ordinary people have noticed this, and they have given us a label for the type: good old boy.

Many of the labels for social types have been introduced this way, as attempts by lay observers to make sense of what they saw around them. Those observers were not trained anthropologists, but that is no reason to dismiss their efforts out of hand. "Our concepts," Immanuel Wallerstein has written, "reflect the evolving social situations in which we live. . . . Many, indeed perhaps most, originate among participants in the 'real world.' And scholars are sometimes among the last, rather than the first, to perceive the utility of these concepts."[7] I doubt that Wallerstein had the good old boy in mind, but he could have said the same thing if he had.

Particularly if a type acquires a label, it is likely to become not merely a social fact but also a psychological and a cultural fact. Along with the label goes a folk version of what Max Weber called an "ideal type," an image of someone who has all the defining characteristics in their pure and unadulterated form, an ideal which real, on-the-ground human beings approximate, to a greater or lesser degree.[8] People carry this image around in their heads, and the label evokes it. The image helps them organize and deal with the reality they encounter. It lets them sort people out and pigeonhole them; it lets them believe they know what to expect from others. And because it is a *shared* image, it helps people communicate with one another.

This is, in short, *useful stuff*. No wonder that people are eager to learn it, that parents teach it to their children, that it passes into the folklore of the group. One of the things people learn, growing up in any culture, is what its social types are, what they look like and how they behave, what to expect from them. We learn this early in life about our own society, largely without thinking about it. If we are immigrants or visitors in another society, we have to learn it all over again before we can function as effectively as a native.

Social types are so useful that people will inevitably construct them. But the way they work is not wholly benign. Sometimes they are just harmless, innocent aids to ordering the blooming, buzzing confusion of experience and to efficient communication. Other times, social types are played for laughs, and everyone can share in the joke, one way or another. But sometimes what we have are vicious stereotypes that have long outlived their usefulness (if, indeed, they ever had any), or that are used to justify discrimination and hard-dealing of various sorts.

Another troublesome aspect of social types is that once people are labeled they find themselves being rewarded in various ways for behaving as the label demands, or being punished for falling short. People who have been well brought-up may evaluate their own performances, and reward and punish themselves. In the extreme case, the role associated with a social type can become part of an individual's identity, part of his sense of *who he is*. We do not need the sociological perspective called labeling theory to tell us that people to whom labels are attached often respond by trying their best to deserve those labels, but labelling theory does tell us that.[9] And this can be true whether the label is a generally admired one or not. I suppose that few would object to someone's thinking of himself as a gentleman and trying to act like one, but what about someone who has been told that he is a redneck, and believes it?

Very much to the point is the discussion of social types most likely to be known to students of Southern life and culture, that by Stanley Elkins, in his book, *Slavery*.[10] Elkins was discussing "Sambo," a character that antebellum whites often thought they saw, at least, when they looked at black men. That role, well played, had its compensations. There were very real rewards for those black men who were willing to live up—or down—to that model.

"Was he real or unreal?" Elkins asked. "What order of existence, what rank of legitimacy, should be accorded him? Is there a 'scientific' way to talk about this problem?" After several stabs at it, Elkins finally concluded that "the most satisfactory of the several approaches to Sambo" is probably that of role theory. In his application of role theory, Elkins was very close to treating Sambo as a social type (although he did not use that phrase), and he could have saved himself a lot of grief if he had begun there.

In this view, individuals are offered "a range of choices in models of behavior and expression, each with its particular style, quality, and attributes": they are offered, in other words, a menu of social types. But culture writes the menu, defines the range of alternatives. We make our character, but we must make it out of the material at hand. Actors, as I said, are rewarded for good performances and punished for bad ones, and there are strong pressures to internalize a role, to make it part of one's self. Indeed, as Elkins put it, "there appears an extent to which we can say that personality is actually made up of the roles which the individual plays." But although "the relationship between the 'role' and the 'self' . . . is intimate," the two are not the same.

If Elkins had emphasized more strongly that Sambo was one slave type in a larger repertoire, and left open the question of how often the role was adopted and how deeply it was internalized, he would have had a less striking, but probably a sounder, argument.

In any case, a great deal that Elkins had to say about Sambo could as easily have been said about other antebellum types, black or white, or for that matter about any social type in any society. A persona "ultimately not an emanation from the proper substance of the men who wore it, but only a . . . garment put on from outside"—that is not Elkins on Sambo, but W. J. Cash on the antebellum planter in the upland South. Like Sambo, the planter-gentleman-aristocrat was a well-defined role that those with the necessary qualifications could indeed "put on." And, although Cash did not say it, it was one that could become so habitual that its wearer felt naked without it.[11]

On the other hand, some roles (and no doubt Sambo was often one of them) are even less than skin-deep, played entirely for immediate advantage. Governor George Wallace tells how he played the dumb hillbilly, while he was in the Army in Colorado, for very immediate advantages indeed:

> [There] was a bunch of girls working at the PX, and me and my buddy [from Mississippi] went in and asked 'em for a can of Brewton's snuff. They asked us what our fathers did and I told 'em my daddy was in the penitentiary for makin' whiskey. They smiled and got all giggly—those gals had found 'em some real live hillbillies. I asked 'em, "How'd you like to go sparkin'?" They agreed to go to a motion picture—a hundred thousand soldiers out there they wouldn't give a date to. They were so gullible.[12]

Where had these young women learned what they thought they knew about hillbillies? Well, they might have heard Homer and Jethro on the radio. They might have read "Li'l Abner" or "Snuffy Smith" in the funny papers. Some years later they could have watched "Hee Haw" on television. Of course they would have known that these pictures of life in the Southern hills were no more accurate than the picture of black life available from "Amos 'n' Andy," but still. . . .

Every society has a battery of social types that its members use to classify one another, but what we might call the economy of social types has been profoundly affected by mass literacy and the mass media of communication. George Tindall has pointed out the importance of "even third-rate creative literature" in understanding mythology.[13] In fact, it is *es-*

pecially third-rate literature that is valuable in understanding social types; and motion pictures, television, and the lyrics of popular music may be more important still. The mass media have proven to be voracious consumers of social types, picking them up, legitimating them, amplifying them, and feeding them back to the audience as categories for thought, sometimes as models to be emulated.

It is obvious why the mass media have such an appetite for social types, and why their treatment of them is so unsatisfying. Television, Ernie Kovacs said once, is called a medium because it is neither rare nor well-done. Limits of time or pages to work with; limits imposed by audience attention spans; limited producer talent, perhaps—all of these combine with insatiable demand for "product" to guarantee that television, like movies, junk novels, and other media of popular culture, will often fall back on the sort of shorthand that a vocabulary of social types provides.[14] So well-known figures, representing various social types, wander in and out. We recognize them immediately; no elaborate or time-consuming description or stage-setting is required.

The Hollywood Western has been a classic example of a genre constructed to a formula using the same basic ingredients over and over. Continuing efforts to develop a Hollywood "Southern," it seems, have foundered in confusion about who the good guys are. The moonlight and magnolias South is not really consistent with the moonshine and motor speedway South, and neither goes well with sado-historical epics like *Mandingo, Slaves,* or the 1965 remake of *Uncle Tom's Cabin.* Hillbilly comedies of the Lum and Abner variety present still another South, as does the Tennessee Williams–Erskine Caldwell school of degeneracy, which one critic suggests does not cohere as a genre because it deals with "flamboyant individuals (often deranged)" instead of stereotypes.[15]

In any case, though, there has been no shortage of stock Southern characters in the movies, even if they have usually been in *different* movies, and most of them have made the transition to television.[16] The redneck villain, for instance, needs no introduction: we remember him from *The Heat of the Night,* where he was beating up Sidney Poitier. We saw him shoot Captain America in *Easy Rider,* and do worse things still in *Deliverance.* Since the death of disco, anybody in a white suit is once again presumably the comic Southern gentleman: Senator Phogbound in "Li'l Abner," Colonel Sanders peddling fried chicken, or Boss Hogg scheming to get the Duke boys. The Dukes themselves are of course good old boys, modeled after Burt Reynolds and Jerry Reed, who in turn remind us of someone seen many times before, whom we cannot quite place. And the syndicated television program "Hee Haw" has been called "a paradigm of essences toward which the phenomenology of the world [is] in continuing approximation," offering a veritable menagerie of Southern social types: gentlemen and ladies, belles and comic hillbillies, good old boys and hillbilly gals.[17]

It is almost conventional to compare popular culture to folk culture unfavorably, and I am going to do it again. It seems to me that the media pick through the rich, flavorsome stew of social types, recognized and chronicled in folk culture, extracting a morsel here, a tidbit there, and feeding them back to us in a gravyless, oversimplified *nouvelle cuisine* version.[18] But that is more an aesthetic judgment than a sociological one.

The media also have a mighty appetite for *new* social types. Spotting emerging types has become a minor industry in twentieth-century America. How many journalistic reputations have been made by describing the habits and appearance of punks, or yuppies, or urban cowboys for *New York* or *Esquire* magazine? How much money has been made on handbooks for aspiring preppies, or even aspiring rednecks?[19] The media identify and validate—perhaps even occasionally create—new social types. Their cultural implications are explored by Phil Donahue and other sages; their representatives appear as characters in situation comedies and, if appropriate, as guests on talk shows. But the novelty value wears off, and some worn-out social types find themselves discarded, like used Kleenex-brand facial tissues.

There is no sinister intent behind this cycle, and in any case it is probably inevitable. It may well merely accelerate a natural process of turnover. By speeding up the introduction of new models and the obsolescence of old ones, the media may even introduce a needed flexibility to our repertoire of social types, to our language, really, of social thought.

But the process certainly introduces an element of *fashion* that was not there before. Nothing is more old-fashioned than yesterday's social types: yuppies, nerds, quiche-eaters, punks—all of those terms will soon sound as hopelessly dated as Klapp's sad sacks and good joes do today. (Quiche-eaters is a little musty already.) Someone today who refers to hippies labels *himself*, as out of it. Beatnik, of course, is even worse.

The real thing, the referents of these labels, may still exist. And the labels themselves may still have currency in various cultural backwaters where the typological fashion is still trickling down, in a way that would have been perfectly familiar to Thorstein Veblen.[20] But the cultural pacesetters will have moved on to something else.

Consider the "urban cowboy" phenomenon. Young blue-collar workers in Houston and elsewhere in the Southwest had been going to cowboy clubs like Gilley's for years before Aaron Latham told *Esquire* readers about it.[21] (Latham's article, incidentally, was coupled with another that called attention to Ralph Lauren's new line of "Western" clothes.) John Travolta made a movie about the phenomenon, based on Latham's article, and cowboy clubs began to spring up in very unlikely places, often replacing the discos that an earlier Travolta movie had inspired. Soon account executives and interior decorators were into cowboy, putting on the superficial trappings with their $200 boots and going off to dance the cotton-eyed joe and ride the mechanical bull, just like *real* urban cowboys. Willie Nelson and Emmy Lou Harris stumbled into respectability. *Playboy*, ever in tune with what's happening now, served up a cowgirl Playmate, Miss January 1982, who volunteered that the Lone Star Chili Parlor was comparable to anything in Paris or Venice.[22]

Where are the urban cowboys of yesterday? Well, the same oil workers can still be found at Gilley's—or maybe somewhere else, now that Gilley's has been overrun by busloads of Midwestern tourists. Wherever they are, they are listening to Conway Twitty sing "Don't Call Him a Cowboy (Until You've Seen Him Ride)." But in California and Manhattan, Tony Lama boots (if nothing else) are in the closet.

The point here is simply that the media these days play a large part in defining the menu of available social types, and in teaching us what they look like. They introduce new types, and they propagate old ones as well.

Playboy's Miss March 1980, for instance, was a classic, photographed both in and out of a hoop skirt. "You might call me the quintessential Southern belle," she suggested. How did this young woman, an orthodontist's assistant, learn that role? How could the Kind of Man Who Reads *Playboy* be expected to know what she was talking about? Well, her favorite movie was *Gone With the Wind*, and she opined that "Scarlett and I are very similar."[23]

Life *does* imitate art. Obviously there were high-spirited belles before Vivien Leigh portrayed Scarlett O'Hara, but *Gone With the Wind* burned that image into the brains of orthodontists' assistants and *Playboy* readers everywhere. There were good old boys before Tom Wolfe wrote about them, but the fact that he *had* written about them, and called one of them "the last American hero," probably had something to do with their prevalence in the Carter White House. Senator Sam Ervin was an original, no doubt about it, but his courtly manners and country wisdom played to another familiar type, and during the Watergate hearings, some of us suspected that he was reading his press clippings, and imitating himself.

What the media have done is to ensure that the Southern gentleman, the belle, the good old boy are nationally advertised Southern types, known and accepted everywhere. More than that: the media have made these types into roles (in the dramatic, not the sociological sense) that many know the lines for and can choose to play, so long as they meet the brute demographic requirements.

Listen to Walker Percy's character, Lancelot Lamar, describe how his wife, after making over his house, made him over as well:

> She didn't restore me exactly, she created me according to some Texas-conceived image of the River Road gentry, a kind of gentleman planter without plantation, a composite, I came to understand, of Ashley Wilkes (himself a creature of another woman of course, an anemic poetic Georgia gent), Leslie Howard (another anemic poetic gent), plus Jeff Davis home from the wars . . . , plus Gregory Peck, gentle Southern lawyer, plus a bit of Clark Gable as Rhett. She even bought my clothes. She liked me to wear linen suits. . . . I even found myself playing up to the role, pacing up and down, stopping now and then to make a legal note at my plantation desk in her Florentine-leather notepad,

John Travolta pretends to be an urban cowboy. He is waiting for a machine that pretends to be a bull. Madolyn Smith pretends to be an up-town Houstonian who is pretending to be a cowgirl. This is from a movie derived from a magazine article based on—oh, never mind. (Museum of Modern Art Film Stills Archive; Paramount Pictures.)

Richard Petty—good old boy, race driver, Republican politician—is living proof that Junior Johnson was not the *last* American hero. He is the real thing. (Compare this to Hollywood's insipid version, shown on page 55.) Note the diffusion to Western North Carolina of urban cowboy headgear. (Bryant McMurray, Photographic Media Services.)

stopping at the cypress cupboard-turned-into-bar to pour a whiskey from crystal decanter into silver jigger, the way Southern gents do in the movies.[24]

Thanks in large part to the media, our system of social types has become more fluid. New types appear and old ones fade. Entry requirements have been relaxed, and the lines are more widely known. But as roles have become more accessible, they have become more shallow—more provisional, situational, contingent. There is often an element of masquerade about it. . . .

The final irony is when the simulation becomes the fact. Robert Sherrill has written about a phenomenon he calls "feedback hillbilly." A Southern country style (in language, say, or music) is picked up by Nashville, routed through Madison Avenue, piped back to the folks who originated it. "Behold, the Synthetic Southerner: a golem who believes in his own myth. . . ."[25]

However they come about, though—even in this media-made form—social types remain realities, on several levels. They signify, in the first place, collections of real people, who resemble one another in ways that could be quantified and measured if we wanted to do it. On a second level, they are popular ideal types: folk generalizations about the kinds of people one is likely to encounter; and some types, for some people, are models to aspire to. Third, in modern society, they often exist as media images: stock characters, no more complicated than they have to be, who are run onstage, perform their limited and predictable function, then exit. Finally, because of their media celebrity, they sometimes exist as roles that individuals can choose to play, from time to time.

All of this is true for all social types in a modern industrial society. But social types identified with a particular subculture or community within a larger society, like racial or ethnic types or the regional types that concern us here, offer an additional complication. When one cultural group looks at another—let us say when a dominant group looks at a minority group—it often sees something different from what that group sees when it looks at itself.[26]

In extreme cases, insiders' and outsiders' typologies may be similar but their evaluations diametrically opposed: one group's heroes are the other's villains; one group's wise men, the other's fools. In other words, a minority's social typology can be *countercultural*, in the strict sense of that word. Sambo looked foolish to antebellum whites; but shift the point of view—and you have something very similar to the traditional African figure of the trickster, Br'er Rabbit, whose defining characteristic is mother-wit. Uncle Tom, as originally painted for white readers, was a saint; needless to say, that has not been his meaning for several generations of blacks. This moral ambiguity in interracial social typing is illustrated, too, by a string of heroic "bad niggers" running from Superfly back to Staggerlee and beyond.[27]

This sort of inversion is the exception. Most often, outsiders, if they think about a group at all, use a simplified version of the group's own social typology to do it with. Indeed, they usually learn the vocabulary in the first place from the group itself. Certainly this has been the case for non-Southerners thinking about the South: all of the labels for white Southern social types originated within the South, applied by Southerners to each other.[28]

But even in cases like this, the same words may mean different things to insiders and outsiders. At the very least, there will be differences in shading and nuance; outsiders will not make the same distinctions as insiders. Insiders invariably feel that even when outsiders have the words, they are missing the music.

The reasons for this are obvious enough. In the first place, any group is more important to its members than to outsiders, and distinctions within it *matter* more to insiders. The difference between lowland and upland South, for instance, so important in Southern history and politics, is largely lost on non-Southerners—like the differences among the many varieties of Baptists.

Moreover, even when two groups deal frequently with one another face to face, power relations and pre-existing images can filter perceptions, in ways that are well-known; they can even shape the reality that is there to be perceived, through the mechanism of the self-fulfilling prophecy.[29] Outsiders often see members of a group in contexts quite different from those in which they see each other: consequently, they do not see the full range of behavior; they may lack information that they need to evaluate what they do see. Is it typical? Is it internalized? Outsiders may not be able to tell, even when group members are actually present in person. Of course, they often *think* they know, and that is the problem. Antebellum whites "knew" Sambo. Those girls in Denver had George Wallace pegged.

And if insiders and outsiders see things differently when they are face-to-face, how much more likely are they to do so when outsiders learn about insiders at second-hand, through the simplified images of the mass media—and some research suggests that is how most non-Southerners initially learn what they think they know about the South. *Before* non-Southerners have any personal experience with the South, they are likely to believe they have learned about it, from the mass media (especially, according to one sample of Pennsylvania college students, from the movies).[30] And what they have learned is likely to structure their perceptions of Southerners when they do get around to meeting some. That is how George Wallace got dates. "They were so gullible," he said. We all are, when we are told things we already think we know.

Of course, non-Southerners will not believe just *anything* about the South. In the 1976 presidential election, one sample of upstate New Yorkers began by evaluating Jimmy Carter very negatively, as a typical Southern politician, a category for which they had very little regard. As their opinions of Carter improved, however, they decided that Carter was not a typical Southern politician; their opinion of Southern politicians did not change at all.[31]

Still, non-Southerners are prepared to believe some very *odd* things about the South. Faulkner's character Gavin Stevens, like George Wallace, spoke of Northerners' "gullibility," of their "volitionless, almost helpless capacity and eagerness to believe anything about the South not even provided it be derogatory but merely bizarre enough and strange enough."[32]

That may be partly Faulkner's fault, though. Edwin Yoder has argued that the South's own "working mythologists," Faulkner definitely included, are responsible for much of the misunderstanding. Yoder writes, for instance, that Tennessee Williams, another culprit,

> was one of us, warts and all, and we loved him for it. But that strange
> Southern blend of sadness, comedy and hysteria seems to have strained the

emotional registers of outsiders. . . . They took Williams too seriously at one level and not seriously enough at another. If you ventured far enough into the steamy, dangerous South, would you really cross a border into a country inhabited by Big Daddies and Maggies, Blanche Duboises and Amanda Wingfields—all counseled, at occasional intervals, by intoxicated Episcopal clergymen? No, not exactly; there was no such alarming place. [But] Williams and the best of the other Southern writers—William Faulkner, Flannery O'Connor, Eudora Welty—succeeded too well, making their imaginary South more vivid than the "real" one.[33]

There has certainly been no shortage of Southerners ready to "tell about the South," and not just the *best* writers of fiction either. For that matter, many working mythologists claim not to be writing fiction at all: they include movie-makers, songwriters, essayists, journalists, historians, even an occasional social scientist.[34] But mythmaking can be a dangerous business when your audience includes outsiders—and it is probably true that until recently there were more non-Southerners than Southerners who wanted to hear about the South, at least in print.

The problem is that outsiders often hear what they want to hear, or at any rate hear something different from what the native mythmaker intends to say. Sometimes they ignore important distinctions; they can be earnest about what is meant to be funny, and laugh at things that are serious.

And it is hard to keep them out of the mythmaking business themselves. When these images escape from captivity, when non-Southerners start to write or talk about the South, based on what they think they have learned from the natives, the results can be strange indeed. That is why Southerners, like many other minority groups, tend to resent it when outsiders talk about them, almost as much as when outsiders ignore them.

At the simplest level the confusion may be merely geographical, as when the Duke boys of Hazzard County run 'shine through the Hazzard County mountains one week and wrestle 'gators in the Hazzard County swamps the next.[35] But the confusion can extend to the social landscape, too. Any Southerner has probably seen the Northern media mistake gentlemen for rednecks, or vice versa.

Walker Percy has had some fun with Hollywood's confused preconceptions about the South. Lance Lamar describes a movie being made at Belle Isle this way:

> The movie was about some people who seek shelter in the great house during a hurricane, a young Cajun trapper, a black sharecropper, a white sharecropper, a Christlike hippie, a Klan type, a beautiful half-caste but also half-wit swamp girl, a degenerate river rat, the son and daughter of the house, even though there are no sharecroppers or Cajuns or even a swamp hereabouts and river rats disappeared with the fish in the Mississippi years ago. And I don't even know what a "half-caste swamp girl" is. I am still unclear about the plot. The Negro sharecropper and the redneck's father, who at first seem to hate each other, form an unlikely alliance to protect the women of the house against rapists of both races. With the help of the Christlike hippie, white and black discover their common humanity. There was something too about the master of the house trying to steal the sharecropper's land, which has oil under it. My only contribution to the story discussions was to point out that the land could not belong to the sharecropper if he was a sharecropper.[36]

My point in all this is not to complain about the unfairness of it all, or even to poke fun at Yankee gullibility, but just to point up some of the dynamics of group relations, dynamics that characterize relations between Southerners and other Americans, just as they have characterized antebellum black-white relations, ethnic relations in Detroit, or even, in some respects, relations between the sexes. It is not given to groups, any more than to individuals, to see themselves as others see them. The best we can hope for in either case is a rough congruence between self-image and others' perceptions, and what either of those has to do with "reality" is an empirical question.

In the following chapters, we will examine the different types of white Southerners to be found in the mass media (easy to do) and in the consciousness of Southerners and non-Southerners (a little harder). As for the different types of Southerners to be found in real life—well, except when we are being "typical" (and most of us, most of the time, are not), that is the hardest subject of all.

Let me close this chapter in the approved Southern manner, with another story, illustrating what a mercurial, many-faceted subject this is, what a thing of smoke and mirrors.

Once again, the narrator is George Wallace, telling of his army days in Colorado. Out of boredom and sheer mischief, he and a buddy from Mississippi amused themselves at their mess-mates' expense by insisting that mountaintops were warmer than valleys because they were closer to the sun, and refusing to believe that there were such things as elevated trains in Chicago:

"We ain't so country we don't know there ain't no trains runnin' along on tracks held up in the air on sticks. We ain't *that* country." Man, their jewglur veins would pop out. They'd run out and get folks from Wyoming and Idaho and bring 'em in there to tell us about them trains. One fella told me, dammit, he was gonna send off and get a picture of those elevated trains to show me. I told him, "Yeah, I know. A trick picture." And they kept tryin' to explain to me about that sun business. A lot of those boys thought you were just ignorant 'cause you came from the South. Got to where they'd jump up every time me and this fella from Mississippi opened our mouths. All we had to do was just *start* to say something. We'd see how fast we could make a fella come up out of his bunk. "By God, that ain't so!"—37

Chapter Two

Gentlemen, Real and Simulated

So far, I have used Southern social types merely as examples, to give some sense of what social types are and how they work. Now we can bring them front and center, introduce them and let them take their bows.

A leading historian of the subject has written that "Southerners were invented as a coherent family of types in the early nineteenth century," which saw the introduction of types that "endure, with modifications, to this day: eccentric planters, duelling Hotspurs, bitchy belles, and amusing rustic bumpkins."[1] This "family of types" is still used by Southerners and non-Southerners alike to think about and to describe different *kinds* of Southerners. There are differences between the home-grown and the exported version: non-Southerners are probably less skilled, or at least less discriminating, in their application, and Southerners tend to feel that some of the details get lost. But by and large when Southerners and non-Southerners use one of these labels they mean roughly the same thing.

Regardless of who is using them, the labels convey very important information. If we are told that someone is a redneck, or a belle, our uncertainty about that person is greatly reduced, if only in a few crucial respects.

In the first place, most social-type labels tell us something about the attitude of the person doing the labelling: admiration, fear, pity, amusement, scorn—there are only a limited number of possibilities. If Bill calls Joe a redneck, we know at least that Bill does not think highly of Joe (with certain ironic exceptions). When we deal in social types, there is an inescapable element of evaluation involved. Most types are seen as either good or bad, sympathetic or unsympathetic.

Types also tend to be seen as strong or weak. Some are competent, independent, in control; others are helpless, dependent, done unto. Darth Vader and Boss Hogg are both bad guys: the difference is that Darth Vader is powerful, and therefore scary; Boss Hogg is an ineffectual bad guy—hence amusing.

It is probably no accident that these two dichotomies, good-bad and strong-weak, seem to underlie social typing: they appear to be fundamental dimensions of human cognition.[2] Cross-tabulating the two dimensions (and omitting the "neutral" categories for simplicity), yields four possibilities: good-strong, bad-strong, bad-weak, and good-weak. And we have four good English words to correspond to these possibilities.

Think of it as melodrama. Good, strong figures are *heroes*. Bad, strong figures are *villains*. Bad, weak figures can be malicious but impotent (like Boss Hogg), or just unsympathetic enough so we feel no sorrow when they come to grief. Either way, they are *fools*. Thus the title of Orrin Klapp's book introducing the concept of social type: *Heroes, Villains, and Fools.*

Klapp's title, you will notice, omitted the category for good, weak types. This is not because the types do not exist: they are, in fact, very familiar. This category (my single, modest contribution here to the theory of social types) is like the fool in one sense: bad things happen to these people, things they are powerless to prevent. But, unlike fools, they are sympathetic characters: we feel sorry for them. I propose to call this category *victims*.

So we have four categories: heroes and villains, fools and victims. All of the social types for white Southern males turn out to fit comfortably in one of the four. But we will see that the fit is less comfortable for white female types; nor do the categories work very well for black types, male or female.

Those two things, sex and race, are two other data that a social type conveys. There are no unisex Southern social types, and precious few biracial ones. Many Southern types, like the lady or the good old boy, carry explicit sexual designations, and all at least imply a sex. In computer jargon, the default redneck is a man (although there are, of course, redneck women). There are hillbilly gals, to be sure, but a hillbilly, unspecified, is male. (By analogy to goats there ought to be "hillnannies.")

White females, as we shall see, have their own roster of heroic, villainous, foolish, and victimized types. But their typology is more complicated than the one for white males. What is seen has probably always depended more on who is looking. Female types are also changing faster. (The social typology for white males is not only simple, it is *stable*; in many respects, it has not changed for over a century.) Finally, some of the female types are more complex—that is, they encode more information—than male types. In particular, they are often age-graded in a way that male types are not. (We will come back to this.)

Race, like sex, has been *so* important in the South that it has generated its own separate typology. Just as some types are explicitly male or female, some are explicitly black or white. East Texas sharecroppers used to sing (and for all I know still do): "I'd rather be a nigger an' plow ol' Beck, / Dan a white hill-billy wid a long red neck."[3] By any reasonable behavioral criteria, there certainly are black hillbillies and even black rednecks, as well as black Southern gentlemen and belles and good old boys, but the labels evoke white images. Blacks have a complex social typology of their own, even more complicated than the one for white females.

It is so complex, in fact, that is strikes me as analytically almost hopeless.[4] I do not believe this is just ethnocentric myopia on my part. Aside from the countercultural aspect of some black types, there is an exaggeration of the usual pattern in which outsiders are blind to distinctions that are important to insiders. In particular, regional differences among blacks are largely lost on whites. Even historical plantation types like Sambo were not restricted in their application to Southern blacks. I suspect that most whites today who think at all of Southern blacks as distinct from non-Southern blacks think of them that way—as Southern *blacks* rather than as black *Southerners*.[5]

Still another analytical problem with black social types is that they seem to have been changing even faster than the ones for white females. Certainly that has been true of their media representations: the media have become downright gun-shy about stereotyping blacks. Many individual whites have, too, at least to judge from a survey in the early 1970s that found very little agreement about "typical Negro traits" among white college students, in marked contrast to twenty and forty years earlier.[6]

A third Great Delimiter, in addition to race and sex, is social class. Each of the types we will examine summons up an image of someone with a particular social standing. This reflects the fact that most of our regional social types were developed and imposed by upper-class Southerners, who wished to distinguish themselves from the lower orders of Southern society.[7] These origins also account, I think, for the fact that the class structure of the mythic South is peculiarly truncated.

We have, for all intents and purposes, two races, and two sexes, and—how many?—social classes. That is an interesting question. The class structure of the actual South is a complex and rapidly changing proposition, but I suggest that white Southern social types can be subsumed in a simple, two-class model, reflecting the view from the top: us or them, genteel or common, upper or lower class.[8]

We will return to this gross oversimplification and the various reasons for pretending that it is adequate. For now, just note that race, sex, and social class set the standards of eligibility, or at least of plausibility, for the various types.[9] Everyone has a menu of social types to choose from, but these factors determine which menu you get. Put another way, each type implies a particular race, gender, and level of gentility. As labels, they convey that information about the person being typed: they tell us, in these terms, what kind of hero, villain, fool, or victim we are dealing with.[10]

One important thing the social-type labels do not tell us. They now imply little or nothing about habitat, urban or rural. All originally described a rural society (what the South was as recently as a generation ago); many once had rustic connotations. A gentleman, for instance, was presumptively a land-owner; a redneck became that by working in the sun. But it is remarkable how effortlessly most of these types have adapted to urban settings—like pigeons. The phrase "urban cowboy," after all, was coined by an *Esquire* reporter: the men he was writing about called themselves just cowboys. Good old boys these days are more likely to be found in filling stations, or insurance offices, than behind a mule, and not just because mules are hard to find. The Southern lady has long since escaped cultivation on the plantation: now she grows wild in the suburbs, and seems as well-adapted to life there as in her original habitat. Only the hillbilly retains the implication of "country," and even he can be urban, but with rural ways. [11]

The new wine seems to go in the old bottles just fine, at least so far as white male types are concerned. Let us begin with those.

If I am right, there are eight basic possibilities: upper-class and lower-class heroes, villains, fools, and victims. All of them turn out to be familiar characters; most have been around for a very long time. All are fixtures in American popular culture, and most Southerners have probably met them in person. I suggest that these are the characters non-Southerners think of, when they think of Southern males *as Southerners.* Equally important: they are what Southern men think of when they think of *themselves* as Southerners.

These types have proven to be strikingly durable. Nearly all were known, in much their present form, by the middle of the nineteenth century. In fact, six of the eight were described, for all intents, in a remarkable book published in 1860, by Daniel R. Hundley, *Social Relations in Our Southern States.* [12]

Hundley was an Alabamian of Virginia parentage, but he wrote his book in Chicago, where he had gone to work for his father-in-law after graduation from Harvard Law School. Hundley was disturbed that "windy Northern demagogues" had confused "the mass of our Free State citizens" by insisting that there were only two kinds of whites in the South, "Poor Whites" and "Cavaliers" (81). In fact, Hundley argued, beneath the descendants of "high-bred English courtier[s]" on the social ladder were "some half-dozen other [white] classes, possessing different degrees of culture and refinement" (10). Hundley meant his book to be a serious ethnography, describing these different sorts of Southerners and setting the record straight.

What Hundley called "classes" he saw as fixed and rigid categories, virtually as castes, not as the combination of social role and observer response that I have been using the phrase "social type" to convey. But three of his chapters describe upper-class types: one turns out to be heroic, one is villainous, and the third is foolish. Three more chapters describe lower-class whites: again, there is a hero, a villain, and a fool.[13] (There were no victims in Hundley's social drama: that type was left to the social typologizing of abolitionists and of a later, more sentimental, generation of Southerners.)

If we can ignore Hundley's theories about the genealogies of these different groups (and I think we can), their defining characteristics become, first, their general social and economic position ("class," in the sociological sense); then, within each class, what would today be called "lifestyle." Both of these were summed up in images that Hundley clearly carried in his head, images that he regarded with admiration, dislike, contempt, or amusement; responses that indicate that we are dealing with a catalog of social types. If we regard Hundley less as an analyst than as a subject himself, presenting us with a gentleman's-eye view of antebellum society, then his book becomes grist for our mill.

The longest by far of Hundley's chapters on the South's white population is the first, devoted to "The Southern Gentleman." The Gentleman has a "natural dignity of manner" and "the utmost self-possession—that much coveted *savoir faire*, which causes a man to appear perfectly at home, whether it be in a hut or a palace." In his manners, he is "remarkably easy and natural, never haughty in appearance, or loud of voice—even when angry rarely raising his voice above the ordinary tone of gentlemanly conversation." He "detest[s] boorishness and vulgarity"; he does not interlard his speech with "Southern provincialisms and Africanisms." And so forth (70–72).

Hundley's picture of the gentleman is utterly conventional, and we have similar sketches from many other hands.[14] This figure was an integral part of the Old South plantation myth.[15] His special habitats, of course, were Virginia and South Carolina, those parts of the antebellum South that had been settled the longest, where a family tradition of gentility could be old enough to pass unquestioned. Outside those areas, Virginians were apparently regarded as gentlemen almost *eo ipso*, and Hundley himself was inordinately proud of his Virginia ancestry.

He was not alone. Joseph G. Baldwin wrote that, in Hundley's Alabama and in Mississippi,

> The franchise of having been born in Virginia and the prerogative founded thereon are . . . patent of honor and distinction. . . . The bare mention is enough. [The Virginian] finds occasion to let the fact be known, and then the fact is fully able to protect and take care of itself. Like a ducal title, there is no need of saying more than to name it; modesty then is a becoming and expected virtue; forbearance to boast is true dignity.

Naturally the Virginian was magnanimous toward those less fortunate. "He never throws up to a Yankee the fact of his birthplace." Virginians carried this refinement so far, Baldwin claimed, that he heard one, "on occasion of a Bostonian owning where he was born, generously protest that he had never heard of it before."[16]

Robert E. Lee, of course, was a real Virginian, and apparently a real gentleman. Or so Allen Tate came to believe when he tried to write Lee's biography. Tate concluded that Lee was a gentleman pure and simple; too pure and too simple, too unlike Allen Tate to hold Allen Tate's attention.[17] What you saw was what you got: Lee was a gentleman through and through. The role was thoroughly internalized, completely unstudied; understand it and you understood the man. It was only natural that when Lee became the premier saint of the white South's civil religion in the decades after the Civil War he also became the epitome of the Southern gentleman.[18]

But Lee had several generations of Virginians behind him. Few would-be gentlemen outside Virginia and South Carolina could claim that kind of breeding, although they did their best. In the rawer parts of the region (that is, in most of the antebellum South), being a gentleman came less naturally and took more work. It also came less naturally for upwardly mobile or aspiring middle-class Southerners who lacked the pedigree or the property to be acknowledged as gentry, by the gentry. We heard from W. J. Cash that many antebellum "gentlemen" were playing a role that was not theirs by right; certainly, as we will see, many self-styled gentlemen believed that other self-styled gentlemen were pretenders.

What has become of the Southern gentleman since Hundley's day? The simple fact that I can write about him without elaborate explanation is proof that he still exists as a social type. The actual figure is as rare as ever, and maybe rarer, but as a culturally defined and transmitted ideal, the Southern gentleman is alive and reasonably well in our mass media, albeit usually in a nineteenth-century context. He is also flourishing in the version of the Old South purveyed by the tourism offices of the Southern states: one brochure, for instance, points to antebellum Arkansas as "a model of grace for all the ages."[19] Lee's cultus has lost some of its vigor, but it still has its devotees, and not only among the brothers of Kappa Alpha.[20] As recently as the 1970s his was the name most often given when white North Carolinians were asked what Southerner they most admired.[21]

This sort of historical notoriety perhaps explains why the gentleman is still a role that most middle-class Southern men can play, at least to the satisfaction of Yankees, whose presence (especially if they are female) often evokes it. Outside historical fiction and drama, however, the Southern gentleman as a heroic social type seems strangely tired and uncertain. We will look at some of the reasons for that in Chapter Five.

The gentleman's villainous counterpart, the evil aristocrat, may be suffering from the same malaise. Here again, we have a character well-established historically, one who lives on vigorously in "period" epics (in such latter-day abolitionist tracts as *Roots* and *Mandingo*, for instance), but one who seems to have few modern descendants.

The upper-class villain has no generally accepted label, but he represents the under-side of the durable plantation legacy: what Hinton Helper called "the lord of the lash."[22] Like the gentleman-hero, the aristocrat-villain was a creature of the antebellum period.[23] As prelude and accompaniment to civil war, the white South's adversaries constructed a portrait of upper-class Southern cruelty and depravity similar in its outlines and its political usefulness to the old British "Black Legend" of the Spanish.[24] Sometimes this portrait was drawn with such emphasis on its more lascivious aspects (the abolitionist Wendell Phillips, for instance, characterized the South as "one great brothel") that we can speculate about its psychological as well as its political functions.[25] For whatever reasons, though, before Appomattox and for some years thereafter, an image was at large of an upper-class Southerner who was downright *evil*.

Oddly enough, Daniel Hundley knew some folks like that. He acknowledged that not all planters were gentlemanly paragons. He, too, depicted an avaricious and cruel upper-class Southerner. Driven by greed,

> the crack of his whip is heard early, and the crack of the same is heard late, and the weary backs of his bondmen and his bondwomen are bowed to the ground with over-tasking and over-toil, and yet his heart is still unsatisfied; for he grasps after more and more, and cries to the fainting slave: "Another pound of money, dog, or I take a pound of flesh!" (132).[26]

This picture is not at all unfamiliar, but these were startling words from the pen of a Southern defender of slavery in 1860: Hundley attempted to cover himself by dubbing this character "The Southern Yankee."

Haughty, domineering, arrogant, and *dangerous:* that is, both bad and powerful. But sometime after Appomattox, that image became primarily an historical one. Some years ago, Howard Odum pointed out that the Southern demagogues of his day, unlike the South's antebellum leaders, were seen by the rest of the country as a collection of posturing blowhards, unpleasant but ineffectual—fools, not villains.[27] No doubt this reflects in part the fact that twentieth-century Southern politicians have been drawn from less lofty social strata than their predecessors, but there have also been actual changes in the regional balance of power. If few members of the Southern elite have lately been objects of fear as well as dislike, it may be because Southerners have in fact been less powerful in the twentieth century than they were in the 1850s; there has been less reason to take them seriously, less use for a Black Legend.[28]

But this in turn may be changing, as a new myth of the South emerges. If the South, as part of an upstart "Sunbelt," once again threatens the Northeast's economic and cultural dominance, upper-crust Southern villains may again figure in our national mythology.[29] In the mid-seventies, a writer in *The New Yorker* tried his hand at mythmaking, sketching a sinister figure called "the Rimster Cowboy" (from "the Southern Rim").[30] It never really caught on as a type, perhaps it was meant to encompass

These evil aristocrats of the Old South are horsing around in *Mandingo.* They are just plain *bad*, and so was the movie. (Museum of Modern Art Film Stills Archive; Dino De Laurentiis.)

Ted Turner can dish it out, but is he *nasty* enough to be an up-scale villain, Sunbelt-style? A Southerner who whips Yankees at their own games may have the makings of a hero. (Turner Broadcasting System.)

everybody from George Wallace to Meyer Lansky, but other mythmakers may be more successful. It seems to me that a number of Southern public figures who would have been dismissed as fools a generation ago are being eyed nervously these days; in time they may develop into full-fledged mythic villains.

Consider a front-page story from the *Wall Street Journal* about Ted Turner's 1985 attempt to acquire CBS. "It's hard to laugh at Turner's operations now," the article said. Turner, head of the Turner Broadcasting System of Atlanta, was described as a latter-day Lord of the Lash: the *Journal* portrayed with horror his "habit of ordering his senior executives to fetch drinks for him" and quoted the chairman of CBS as telling a press conference that Turner was not "moral enough" to run a major network.[31] These reassessments stopped with the failure of the takeover attempt, and they might not have worked anyway: Turner may be too obviously good-natured to be a plausible bad guy. But the very model of a modern Southern villain is right there on the network he tried to take over, in the person of J. R. Ewing of "Dallas."

Which brings us to the third sort of upper-class Southern figure: the *comic* gentleman, or white-suited buffoon. This is the character—call him "the Colonel" for short—toward which the Southern gentleman-aristocrat, whether hero or villain, seems inevitably to tend these days, like radium becoming lead. But the type was already well-known in the antebellum South. Hundley wrote about him in the figure of the "Cotton Snob," an expression whose application he did not restrict to actual growers of cotton. By "displays of arrogance and ill-breeding," Hundley wrote, "the Cotton Snob . . . renders himself both ridiculous and contemptible; and, what is more and worse, brings a reproach upon the true Gentlemen of the South" (170). Since Hundley was mightily concerned to help his reader distinguish between true Gentlemen (like himself) and the South's false or mock gentlemen, Southern Yankees and Cotton Snobs, he listed a great many identifying marks: the Cotton Snob, for instance, "seeks every opportunity to talk about 'my niggers,' [while] a Southern Gentleman rarely if ever says *nigger*" (170).

We have become so accustomed to self-help books that it is difficult not to read this as a clever book of etiquette, telling its reader not just how to recognize a gentleman, but how to *be* one. Hundley, though, saw his book as nothing of the kind. He aspired to be the Audubon of antebellum society, not its Emily Post. In his view, a Southern Yankee could no more become a Gentleman than a vulture could become an eagle, because the distinction was hereditary and immutable.

Some of the identifying marks were physical. The true Gentleman, Hundley wrote, is "usually of aristocratic parentage," and with his "faultless pedigree [the Gentleman] is usually possessed of an equally faultless physical development. His average height is about six feet, yet he is rarely gawky in his movements, or in the least clumsily put together; and his entire *physique* conveys to the mind an impression of firmness united to flexibility" (27–28). The Southern Yankee, on the other hand, more often of Scotch or Irish extraction, or from the humbler orders of English society, is "muscular, heavy-jawed, beetle-browed, and possessed of indomitable energy." The "best specimens of the genuine Southern Yankee are to be found in Georgia [where] they grow to enormous sizes, and seldom stand under six feet in their stockings, often, indeed, reaching six feet and a half" (81–82, 157).[32] The Cotton Snob presumably looks like the Southern Yankee; "in nine cases out of ten" his father was one (165).

Most of all, though, the Cotton Snob was "ridiculous and contemptible." Here is the tip-off that we are dealing with a fool: he is not even dangerous. This character can be a failed villain like Boss Hogg of "The Dukes of Hazzard," a pompous windbag like Senator Phogbound in "Li'l Abner," or an amiable trademark like Colonel Sanders: whatever else he is, he is basically harmless (that is, weak) and he does not engage our sympathy enough to keep us from laughing at him. As these examples indicate, he is certainly still around (and it should be noted that he seems to be at least as popular with white Southern audiences as with Northern ones, presumably because Southerners recognize the type being caricatured). He is approximately a white version of Kingfish in "Amos 'n' Andy," and there is little else to be said about him.

But there is a great deal to be said about the fourth genus, the good-but-weak victim, starting with the observation that examples are not easy to find. Hundley offered none at all. In general, upper-class victims have been rare in American mythology: presumably a society that values acquisition finds it hard to sympathize with the problems of the upper crust. When we are asked to pity rich people (in country music, for example), they are often poor folks who have *become* rich, and found that being rich is not all it is cracked up to be.

Moreover, there are special problems with the image of the upper-class *male* victim, especially a Southern one. In our regional social typology, the combination of goodness and male weakness seems to be unstable. Weaklings often forfeit the sympathy that could make them victims; without that sympathy, they are simply fools. This near-equation of masculine virtue and strength is of course a warrior ethic, and Bertram Wyatt-Brown's fascinating study of the concept of honor in the Old South could probably help us to understand it better.[33] Like the rest of the orientation Wyatt-Brown describes, it has coexisted uneasily with some aspects of Evangelical Protestantism.[34] In particular, the "suffering servant," the hero-victim (almost an amalgam of the crucified Christ and the defeated Lee) is a figure alien to this view, and, not incidentally, one with a particular appeal to women.

Gentleman-victims, when we do find them, usually partake of this quality. Most are men who are too fine, too sensitive to live—or at least to live and compete with Snopeses. They are overbred Ashley Wilkeses. Tennessee Williams has given us several examples; in Lancelot Lamar's father, Walker Percy has given us another: "Poet Laureate he was of Feliciana Parish, so designated by the local Kiwanis, lying on his recliner on the deep shaded upper gallery dreaming over his history manuscript, dreaming not so much of a real past as what ought to have been and should be now and might be yet: a lovely golden sunlit Louisiana of bayous and live oaks and misty savannahs, Feliciana, a happy land of decent folk and droll folkways and quiet backwaters, the whole suffused by gentle Episcopal rectitude."[35]

That there is something unmanly in victimization is indicated by the fact that these good-but-weak figures merge into the basically comic type of the small-town Southern homosexual. Florence King, a very funny (but treacherous) guide in these matters, has written in *Southern Ladies and*

Gentlemen about several varieties, including the one who "behaves like the classic belle every Southern woman wants to be" and is consequently adored and protected by the ladies of the garden club.[36] It is only to be expected that Lancelot Lamar's father, that gentle man, should have been cuckolded by Lancelot's Uncle Harry, a Schenley salesman.

The gentlemanly style can easily be misperceived, unless it is coupled with unmistakable strength, as indicated, for instance, by valor in combat. As King puts it: "Too much gallantry, especially in this day and age, can seem effeminate because it takes on the anachronistic qualities of a minuet. Fussing over women is a risky business; a man who does too much of it becomes simply fussy."[37]

This is not a problem for the other males in this typology. Nobody ever called the good old boy, the redneck, or the hillbilly *fussy.* Let us examine them, in the next chapter, before we have a look at the womenfolk of the South.

Chapter Three

Common Men

Daniel Hundley, our guide to antebellum Southern society, examined the white lower orders of that society with somewhat less enthusiasm but just as much detail as his own, more genteel social environs.[1] In his treatment of the non-genteel white males of the Old South, again we find the familiar triad of hero, villain, and fool; beneath his descriptions of the Southern Yeoman, the Southern Bully, and Poor White Trash, we can discern the direct ancestors of types we know today as the good old boy, the redneck, and the hillbilly.

Hundley's Southern Yeomanry, for instance, can be found, essentially unchanged, in any number of country songs, many of them by Merle Haggard, Charlie Daniels, and Hank Williams, Jr. "Nearly always poor, at least so far as this world's goods are to be taken into the account" (193), their only "inheritance . . . is the ability and the will to earn an honest livelihood . . . by the toilsome sweat of their own brows" (192). But (or, perhaps, consequently) this figure exhibits "a manly independence of character"; he will not "under any circumstances humiliate himself to curry favor with the rich or those in authority." He is courageous, never wounded from behind (199).

There is an element of good-natured fun in this fellow. He is fond of turkey-shoots (199), frolics and family gatherings (216), political barbecues (201), and the drinking of home-brewed spirits, "said to be both wholesome and harmless, if taken in moderation" (203). He is "seldom troubled with dyspepsia, or melancholy, or discontent with his humble lot" (198).[2] The antebellum yeoman was not often a slaveholder, although he aspired to be one; when he was, he worked the fields with his slaves, and Hundley observed with amusement that he was "not offended when they call[ed] him familiarly by his Christian name" (197).[3]

I submit that we have here what amounts to an authentic, indigenous working-class hero: positive, independent, competent, and strong. This type, long present in fact and in the self-image of ordinary Southerners, has often been overshadowed in the mass media by various villains, fools, and victims. But in the last generation, it has emerged from regional obscurity, and has even been "commodified" (an ugly word that has nothing to do with plumbing). I refer to the emergence on the national scene of the good old boy.

To repeat: something similar has been around for a long time. Hundley was describing him, and he is also pretty much the same chap W. J. Cash wrote about in *The Mind of the South* as the "hell of a fellow."[4] But in the wake of Tom Wolfe's 1965 *Esquire* article portraying Junior Johnson, a North Carolina stockcar racer, as "the last American hero," the mass media swarmed on the good old boy *type* that Wolfe had identified and labeled with an indigenous label.[5] "Suddenly," as Florence King put it, "there was *something* called a Good Ole Boy instead of men who had always been called Good Ole Boys."[6]

Explaining what good old boys were soon became a lucrative sideline for Southern writers, some of whom, surely, were playing games with Northern gullibility. Florence King, for example, claimed to be describing the type for *Harper's* readers in 1974: among the identifying marks were "a callous on his trigger finger . . . , baggy suntans, a white shirt open at the neck with the cuffs rolled back one turn, an enormous carved belt buckle of the *Gott und Reich* variety decorated with horns or antlers, white socks, and Marine Corps-issue shoes with thick soles and cleats." She shot her credibility entirely by asserting that nearly *all* Southern males qualified.[7] Johnny Greene, also writing in *Harper's*, did not go quite that far, but implied that President Carter was one, which is patently ridiculous.[8] *Harper's* identified Greene as "a free-lance writer based in Alabama," but since he griped that "it is not easy to penetrate [good old boys'] inscrutable colloquialisms," we must suspect that he is not the man to turn to for reliable information.[9]

So many Southerners undertook to explain things that Walker Percy complained: "If I hear one more northerner ask about good ol' boys and one more southerner give an answer, I'm moving to Manaus, Brazil, to join the South Carolinians who emigrated after Appomattox and whose descendants now speak no English and have such names as Senhor Carlos Calhoun. There are no good ol' boys in Manaus."[10] And with so much misinformation about, it is no wonder Yankees were confused. For them, in the mid-1970s, "good old boy" became simply a convenient term for a white Southern male one approved of who was not courtly enough to be a gentleman, and it retained that simple meaning until it became something of a derogatory label, about midway through the Carter administration.[11]

In the South, however, the phrase has retained more precise connotations. It began as a term of approbation among working-class Southerners, and it has continued to mean someone with qualities that working-class Southerners admire. Even after it appeared in Rebel Yell whiskey ads and political analyses of the Carter White House, even after all manner of middle-class Southern males laid claim to the title (a subject we will come back to in Chapter Five), the phrase remained something more than just an expression of affection.

Ingram Parmley, a sociologist in Florence, South Carolina, cast down his bucket where he was; in an article called "Stalking the Good Old Boy," he listed a number of the type's admirable and essential traits.[12] His research-based conclusions were roughly the same as the less systematic observations of Roy Blount, Jr. That acute analyst of Southern folkways (sometimes mistakenly regarded by Northerners as a humorist) has written that "if somebody is a solid, reliable, unpretentious, stand-up, companionable, appropriately loose, joke-sharing feller, with a working understanding of certain bases of head-to-head equal footing, you say, 'You know, he's a good old boy.'"[13]

Such a fellow has a lot of virtues, but generally in moderation. He is decent, but not priggish.[14] "A good old boy will take advantage of another good old boy when he has to," Blount writes, "and will help him out when he can. He will also take some creative pride in the way he does the one thing and the other and mixes the two together."[15] The good old boy is

Just good old boys, I: Burt and Jerry with friend. The Bandit and Cledus relax with Fred, in *Smokey and the Bandit.* (Museum of Modern Art Film Stills Archive; Universal Studios.)

Just good old boys, II: Burt and Kris with friend. Billy Clyde and Shake go to the altar with Barbara Jane, in *Semi-Tough.* (Museum of Modern Art Film Stills Archive; United Artists.)

not just a social type, but a *sociable* type: good old boys seem typically to travel in pairs—Burt and Jerry, Bo and Luke, Moe and Joe, Ham and Jody.[16]

Some attitudes and interests, although not required, are more *appropriate* than others. "Generally speaking," according to Blount, "it is harder to be recognized as a good old boy if you have a passion for racial justice, or an interest in, say, art, than if you have a passion for stock-car racing or an interest in, say, veterinary medicine—harder, even, than if you have a passion for racial *in*justice, or an interest in, say, getting drunk and bringing a live alligator into a public place to see what will happen."[17]

But here we are getting rather far afield. There can be an element of rowdiness about the good old boy, to be sure. As Larry King has pointed out, "when people designate somebody as a good ol' boy the sentence has to start something like, 'Well, now, Bubba, he may beat his wife some and burn a few barns when he's drankin', and there's the time he shot his little boy's eye out with a BB gun and all that—but he sure is a *good* ol' boy.' "[18] But when we confront actual *malice*, we are dealing with another working-class social type, the redneck villain.

For the distinction between good old boy and redneck, I call on no less an authority than Billy Carter. He defined a good old boy as "somebody that rides around in a pickup truck . . . and drinks beer and puts 'em in a litter bag. A redneck's one that rides around in a truck and drinks beer and throws 'em out the window."[19] The redneck has an outlaw quality that the good old boy lacks, although the distinction is not hard and fast. Some good old boys find that redneckery has a certain appeal, and they take it up, in some phases of the moon. Social types are like that.[20]

But the redneck *type*, as distinct from the men who more or less inhabit it, is an undeniable villain, "one of the most distinctive, disgusting characters of our time" (as F. N. Boney summarized it in the early 1970s). This is "the pale beast of Dixie, who stalks Negroes, Yankees, Federal officials, United Nations representatives, and all the other good guys. He looms large on stage, screen, radio, and television"—never larger than when Boney was writing—and his "beefy, bestial image is deeply embedded in the national mind."[21]

If Hundley's Yeoman was clearly the ancestor of the good old boy, the redneck is equally recognizable in Hundley's sketch of the Southern Bully: "a swearing, tobacco-chewing, brandy-drinking Bully, whose chief delight is to hang about the doors of . . . tap-rooms, to fight chicken cocks, to play Old Sledge, or pitch-and-toss, chuck-a-luck, and the like, as well as to encourage dog-fights, and occasionally to get up a little raw-head-and-bloody-bones affair on his own account." This creature is a uniquely Southern type, Hundley asserted: "in all the world else his exact counterpart is no where to be found" (223–24).[22]

Hundley exercised his considerable powers of description at the Bully's expense (239–40). His attire, for instance, "is usually loose-fitting, dirty, tobacco-stained, liquor-stained, and grease-stained." Naturally, he wears a wool hat, "with a limp flapping brim, battered crown, dirty and fuzzy." David Allan Coe would have recognized this long-haired redneck: his hair is "habitually matted and unkempt," his beard likewise: it "grows in great luxuriance all over his face, or else in ragged patches here and there. . . ." Warming to his subject, Hundley wrote that the Bully's "speech is fouler than his breath." Not only can he "use more obscene language than the vilest pimp," he "can utter more blasphemy in a single hour" than a "whole mess" of Northern freethinkers in a week. "It is wonderful, indeed, what a gift of gab the fellow possesses; what a multitude of strange and agglomerated oaths he can interlard his discourse with."

Always fair-minded, however, Hundley allowed in the Bully's defense that "he is rarely ever a downright thief, and seldom murders in cold blood, and never attempts to make a dishonest living by swindling the innocent and helpless"—unlike some Yankees Hundley could name, and did (242).[23]

Hundley displayed an intimate acquaintance with tavern life, acquired no doubt in the interests of science.[24] The Southern tavern was the Bully's natural habitat (225). In this "peculiar institution," Hundley wrote, the Bully "delights to lounge and drink, drink and lounge, and lounge and drink again, until he is fitly prepared for bets, brawls, oaths, blasphemies, quarrels, bruises, stabbings, shootings, manslaughters, murders; for in all these things he is more or less an adept" (225, 232). The Bully is "a valiant Southerner . . . able and prepared—cocked and primed, in his own vernacular—to flog the entire North" (224), a chance he got, of course, within a year of the publication of Hundley's book.

Thus, a gentleman's view of the antebellum redneck. For men in wool hats hanging around the tavern, substitute men in farm machinery caps hanging around the filling station, or (the Southwestern version) men in cowboy hats hanging around the honkytonk, and (I submit) you have today's version.

The redneck's essential characteristic is *meanness.* The good old boy will certainly fight if he has to, and may sometimes fight from sheer high spirits, but the redneck fights because he wants to *hurt* somebody, often somebody helpless. When Raymond Rodgers analyzed country songs about rednecks, he found that violence figured in seventy percent of them.[25] The redneck's violent image was well-established long before the civil-rights era, but it was polished and reinforced by the murders and brutality of that period. Americans who might have been expected to see working-class Southern whites as sturdy yeomen, or as downtrodden wretched of the earth, or at least as harmless, grotesque rustics, were persuaded otherwise by what they saw on the evening news. The villain, in other words, came center-stage and shouldered aside the hero, victim, and fool.

In some circles, this was the dominant view of the working-class white Southern male in the 1960s, and it is not surprising that the revaluation of the early 1970s evoked deep suspicion. In *Harper's*, Florence King (who surely knew better) suggested that a harmless and actually rather sad song called "Red Necks, White Socks and Blue Ribbon Beer" might become America's "Horst Wessel," and Richard Goldstein wrote in 1973 that "There is something utterly sinister about the image of Richard Nixon inviting Merle Haggard to sing at the White House."[26] It is easy to see why Goldstein felt that way: he went on to write that "I can never encounter a white Southerner without feeling a murderousness pass between us. As though, whatever his personal instincts, his ethnic history predisposes him to regard castration and rape as his prerogatives."

However exaggerated these responses may be, the redneck has cer-

Redneck villains.

Sidney Poitier is in a heap of trouble with this villain, in *The Heat of the Night*. (Museum of Modern Art Film Stills Archive; United Artists.)

Time to blow away the scum: it's all over for Peter Fonda's kind, in *Easy Rider*. (Museum of Modern Art Film Stills Archive: Columbia Pictures.)

tainly established his credibility as a villain, when all that is called for is physical menace. Because his innate meanness is so well-known and widely understood he gets a lot of television and movie roles, and one has to suspect that the absence of any sort of regional Anti-Defamation League may help, too. Examples are legion. I have already mentioned *The Heat of the Night, Easy Rider,* and *Deliverance,* at your local theater. On television, "Rockford Files" reruns include one starring a sort of down-home Manson Family; one episode of "Charlie's Angels" takes place in a sinister Southern town where everyone, including the sheriff, is up to no good; and fans of "Happy Days" will recall what happens when the Fonz goes on a sit-in. Some of the most imaginative treatments can be found in low-budget productions of the *Texas Chain Saw Massacre* genre. One recent example, as summarized by Dallas drive-in movie critic Joe Bob Briggs, features "four creepolas" whose favorite pastimes include "playing with their killer pit bulldog" and "blowing away Mason jars with sawed-off shotguns." In the finale, this "maniac zombie redneck tribe" is subdued by a band of preppy heroes armed with deer rifles.[27]

If the redneck's principal characteristic is *meanness,* another social type is notorious for his *laziness.* This character is usually distinguished from the rest of the white working class in one or more of a number of ways.

In fact, he and his are often regarded as another social class, especially by those who might otherwise be grouped with them—that is, by industrious and competent yeomen, who call them what Hundley called them: "poor white trash."[28] Hundley, to his credit, shared this view, and did not see the distinction between yeomen and trash simply as one between well-behaved and dissolute underlings. As the name "trash" implies, however, the distinction is as much moral as economic.[29]

Such folks are often set apart geographically as well: they are supposed to be especially common in remote and mountainous regions of the South, which has given rise to another generic label: we are talking here about the *hillbilly.*[30] Within the South, "hillbilly" still has an Appalachian or Ozark connotation (Appalachia has always served as the South's "South"), and the epithet of choice for comic or contemptible poor folks of the lowlands has been "trash." But that is one of those distinctions that get lost on non-Southerners, or so we may surmise from the fact that white Southern migrants to the upper Midwest are called hillbillies, even though they tend to come from the flatlands of Mississippi and thereabouts.[31]

Just as rednecks seem to be the last remaining identifiably ethnic villains, so hillbillies appear to be the last acceptable ethnic fools. Poor Southern whites have amused non-Southerners and upper-class Southerners alike since the days of Robert Beverley and William Byrd, going on three hundred years ago, and Hundley was working in a tradition already well-established when he drew his unkind portrait.[32] He vigorously rejected any suggestion that the Poor Whites' degradation had any relation to slavery. (He chalked it up to his customary explanatory variable, heredity: their ancestors came, he said, from "the poor-houses and prison-cells of Great Britain" [258].[33]) But his sketch was as harsh as any Northern critic's.

Even in Hundley's time these folks—sandhillers, crackers, rag-tag-and-bobtail—were said to live off by themselves, particularly "in hilly and mountainous regions . . . far removed from the wealthy and refined settlements" (258). They lived in log cabins, with their dogs and large families, each with a "half-dozen of dirty, squalling, white-headed little brats" (260, 264–65). A family, Hundley wrote, "pretends to cultivate" its small garden plot, but in fact subsists on the "wild hogs, deer, wild turkeys, squirrels, raccoons, [and] opossums" that its menfolk bring in from the woods for sustenance or for barter (260).

Their "chief characteristic" was even then laziness. According to Hundley: "They are about the laziest two-legged animals that walk erect on the face of the Earth. Even their motions are slow, and their speech is a sickening drawl . . . ; while their thoughts and ideas seem likewise to creep along at a snail's pace" (262). Very little of their time was spent in economically productive or uplifting activity. "All they seem to care for, is, to live from hand to mouth; to get drunk, provided they can do so without having to trudge too far after their liquor; to shoot for beef; to hunt; to attend gander pullings; to vote at elections; to eat and to sleep; to lounge in the sunshine of a bright summer's day, and to bask in the warmth of a roaring wood fire, when summer days are over." (262–63)

The Poor White Trash were illiterate, of course, and superstitious (265–

67). Their men drank far too much "'bust-head,' 'rot gut,' or some other equally poisonous abomination" (268). Their women dipped snuff and sometimes even smoked pipes (264).[34] Professing to be puzzled about their part in the divine plan, Hundley speculated tongue in cheek that they were placed on earth to vote for his political party, and claimed that some East Tennesseans were still voting for Andrew Jackson in 1860 (265–66).[35]

They were recognizable on sight: "Lank, lean, angular, and bony, with flaming red, or flaxen, or sandy, or carroty-colored hair, sallow complexion, awkward manners, and a natural stupidity or dullness of intellect that almost surpasses belief." Although this spectacle was "a very pitiable sight to the truly benevolent," it was "a ludicrous one to those who are mirthfully disposed"—among whom I fear we must number Hundley (264).

This image has been kept alive from the literature of Southwestern humor in the nineteenth century to the mass media of the twentieth.[36] Perhaps nowhere has it been more prominent than in hillbilly music, which served up a remarkable collection of ridge-runners and skillet-lickers before it moved to Nashville, changed its name to "country and western," and got respectable.[37]

Building on this indigenous tradition, Hollywood brought these images to a national audience, and television has done the same. In the late 1960s, there was an average of six "Southern" shows per season on prime-time television, nearly all of them rural situation comedies like "The Beverly Hillbillies," "Gomer Pyle," and "Mayberry RFD." CBS, hoping to attract a younger, more urban audience, cancelled three of these programs in 1971 while they were still in the top twenty nationwide, but they survive in syndication. As a matter of fact, *all* of the early Southern sitcoms were still syndicated as late as 1981.[38] And you can't keep a good genre down: It made a comeback in the late seventies with such specimens as "The Dukes of Hazzard," "Carter Country," and "The Misadventures of Sheriff Lobo."

Not all of the characters on these programs are comic hillbillies. Sheriff Andy of Mayberry, for instance, is a more intelligent and admirable figure than, say, Sheriff Roscoe P. Coltrane of Hazzard County. But the comic figures are certainly present, and very appealing to viewers. It seems, for example, that the five most popular episodes of "The Andy Griffith Show" are the five in which Ernest T. Bass, the mad hillbilly, appears.[39]

Some have taken exception to these portrayals. John Egerton and Frye Gaillard, for instance, objected to Al Capp's representations of "dim-witted yokels and pig-sty-wallowing ignoramuses" in "Li'l Abner."[40] David Whisnant has complained about Dogpatch, too, and darkly suggested that "Hee Haw" and "Green Acres" and "The Beverly Hillbillies" are part of "a broader pattern of cultural imperialism."[41] James Branscome found the hillbilly humor of the late sixties sitcoms "the most intensive effort ever exerted by a nation to belittle, demean, and otherwise destroy a minority people within its boundaries"—strong words, indeed, when one considers the competition.[42]

Not all observers have gone that far: some have pointed to positive aspects of media portrayals of hillbillies, and others have noted the awkward fact that such programs have bigger audiences in the South than elsewhere.[43] But Roy Blount once called attention to a *TV Guide* listing for "The Misadventures of Sheriff Lobo" that read "A dimwitted hillbilly inadvertently gets involved in an armored-car robbery," and asked pointedly whether any other ethnic label today would be preceded by the adjective "dimwitted" in a national magazine.[44] It is a fair question.

Once we recognize that "hillbilly" *is* an ethnic label, and a generally derogatory one, many vistas open up. I have already suggested some parallels between "The Dukes of Hazzard" and "Amos 'n' Andy"; Roy Blount suggests that we think of "Hee Haw" as a white-face ministrel show.[45] (But he points out that "Hee Haw" does at least demonstrate that Southerners have forms of entertainment other than reckless driving.)

Poor Southern whites, obviously, have not been lucky in their portraiture. If not seen as vicious redneck brutes, they have often as not been figures of fun. Even when they have received sympathetic treatment from outsiders, as heroes or as victims, that treatment has often been condescending or self-serving, and for all its gritty and self-conscious "realism" it has usually been essentially romantic.

What could be called the WPA Tradition, for instance, has attempted to portray Southern working-class men and women as victims of adversity, and sometimes as heroes struggling against it. *Southern Exposure* magazine and movies like *Norma Rae* stand in a line of such efforts that goes back at least to the thirties. Erskine Caldwell has always claimed that he was working this vein, although his readers have persisted in seeing Jeeter Lester and the others as too repellent to be good victims. Caldwell's and Margaret Bourke-White's documentary volume, *You Have Seen Their Faces*, illustrates this problem: a fundamental lack of sympathy with the characters undercuts its Marxist message.[46] (Much more effective, in my view, is James Agee's collaboration with Walker Evans, *Let Us Now Praise Famous Men.*)[47] Another example, from the same era, is a movie called simply *The Southerner* that shows the trials and triumphs of an East Texas sharecropping family. Despite cinematography by Jean Renoir and a screenplay partly by William Faulkner, *The Southerner* remains didactic melodrama. (It also seems to remain perpetually on late-night television.)[48]

Often, the artists and journalists responsible for these portraits have been non-Southern, and for the most part the images they have dealt in have been left-wing agitprop, with adversity taking the shape of capitalism, or at least of evil upper-class figures. One exception to both of these generalizations was the group of Southerners who wrote *I'll Take My Stand;* their product, with its agrarian hero-victim, was agitprop, indeed, but not exactly left-wing.

But whether imposed from the right or from the left, all of these images have been imposed from outside or above or both, and few have achieved any popular resonance, in the South or outside it. Until recently, the plain folk of the South have generally been viewed unsympathetically by other Americans, North and South, with no political axe to grind.[49] In particular, convincing lower-class *male* victims have been rare birds in our mythical menagerie, although not for want of mythmakers' trying. Why is this?

Some of the same problems that tend to make the upper-class male victim an unsatisfying type are at work here, too. Victimization tends to be seen as *unmanly*, and therefore foolish, in men. A male fool *is* someone to whom things just happen, often unpleasant things. Boss Hogg tries to work his evil will, but is always outwitted, frustrated, and discomfited. Lower-class fools, hillbillies, are basically too lazy even to try. To them, too, things just happen. "They have only themselves to blame," we say, echoing a regional ethic of individualism.[50]

Are we reluctant to sympathize with unfortunate males, to the point of denying that they exist except as fools? Well, yes and no. The story is told (perhaps it is even true) that Governor Folsom of Alabama once told some of his supporters that his opponents were going to bait a trap for him with some good-looking woman. "And, friends"—a pause, and a rueful shake of the head—"they're gonna catch Big Jim every time." Some sorts of weakness are less effeminate than others.

Samuel Johnson said once that sins of excess are no less sinful than sins of insufficiency, but that most of us find them easier to sympathize with, and here is a case in point. A man victimized by a woman's charms— in effect, by an excess of masculinity—is less foolish than one victimized by his deficiency. Big Jim's weakness was not unmanly, so Alabamians laughed *with* him, not at him. No doubt many prayed for him; certainly many voted for him.

It is not only an excess of masculinity that can excuse a loser, either. Almost any kind of excess will do, as a line of victim-heroes reaching from Hank Williams to Elvis Presley attests. What one student of these matters has called the "sex, sin, booze, divorce syndrome" in country music is about *that* kind of weakness.[51] ("I know it's wrong, but I'm weak.") Insufficiency, on the other hand, creates fools, not victims. Too little energy reminds us of Junior Samples, lying in the front yard with the hound dogs. Too little intelligence—maybe Boss Hogg. Too little ruthlessness, and you have Ashley Wilkes, or worse. None of these men is destroying himself in a manly way; each is setting himself up to be mistreated *by others*. Many Southerners have traditionally regarded that as the providential destiny of blacks, and of women.

Chapter Four

Ladies and Other Women

The eight-fold scheme of hero-villain-fool-victim, genteel and common, can also be used to order white Southern female types, but it does not work so neatly—and that tells us some interesting things about how our collective images of Southern men and women are different.

For instance, the male types sort themselves out one to a cell. There are different *kinds* of good old boy, to be sure. (See Florence King's amusing list in *Southern Ladies and Gentlemen* for a start.[1]) But each is recognizably a variation on the same basic theme, not a separate type in its own right. Female types, on the other hand, are far more numerous, and often there are several distinct types in the same cell.

The reason for this is that the female types are more differentiated; they convey more information than the male types do. For instance, the male types tell us very little about age.[2] They can apply to almost any post-pubertal male of the right social class. We can distinguish young gentlemen from old gentlemen, but the adjectives do not produce impossibilities like "old yuppie," or even incongruities like "young fogey" or "old hippie" (the title, by the way, of a country song). The "old" in good old boy has nothing to do with age. A redneck can be virtually any age, and so can a hillbilly. But an "old belle" is grotesque, if not impossible. The belle and the Southern *grande dame* differ qualitatively, in ways that young and old gentlemen do not. Hillbilly gals and grannies are not just points on a continuum either.

In addition, although female social types can certainly be sorted into heroes, villains, fools, and victims, the relation of those categories to the good-bad and strong-weak dimensions is not as straightforward as it is for male social types.

Tomorrow is another day—but Vivien Leigh's portrayal of Scarlett O'Hara goes on and on. . . . (Museum of Modern Art Film Stills Archive; Metro-Goldwyn-Mayer.)

Scarlett has inspired countless imitations. This example is from a Helena, Arkansas, tourist brochure. (Helena Advertising and Tourist Promotion Commission.)

Consider, for instance, the upper-class Southern female figures, the various sorts of Southern lady. Like her consort, the gentleman, the lady had her origins in the antebellum plantation myth. Like him, when she was good, she was very, very good, and she is so well-known that we need not dwell on her lineaments here. As Anne Firor Scott summarized it in her groundbreaking book, the Southern lady could be quite simply "the most perfect example of womankind on earth."[3] And the Southern belle, her larval form: "Beautiful, graceful, accomplished in social charm, bewitching in coquetry, yet strangely steadfast in soul, she is perhaps the most winsome figure in the whole field of our fancy."[4]

But unlike the gentleman-hero, the lady-heroine does not have to be strong. Indeed, as a rule, she should *not* be powerful or strong in conventional, "manly" ways—there are no Valkyries or amazons in the mythic South.[5] Largely for this reason, it seems to be almost obligatory in some circles to disparage the Southern lady, and especially the belle. Margaret Ripley Wolfe has written, for instance, that "The image of the southern lady . . . still impedes the development of Southern women," and has called on her fellow historians to "smash the white idol of the southern home."[6] And Gail Godwin has exhorted readers of *Ms.* magazine to work for "that happy day when all constricting, debilitating stereotypes—including that of 'The Southern Belle'—are relegated to the archives of human evolution."[7]

If the point is that these social types are artificial and confining, I would not disagree: all social types are, to a degree, and no doubt these are more than most. I would venture to observe, though, that Southern ladies need not be submissive or dependent, as some of their detractors seem to assume. Some are, but others are not.[8] Florence King's typology of older ladies is arrayed precisely on our "weak–strong" dimension: from the fluttery and helpless Dear Old Thing to the sturdy, competent Rock to the imperious Dowager.[9] Among belles, too, there is a range in this respect: Melanie, the delicate flower, is an almost necessary foil for the hellcat, Scarlett (who has been described as "J.E.B. Stuart in drag").[10] Pauline Rose Clance, a clinical psychologist, argues that Southern ladies can be accorded considerable power in practice, so long as they pay symbolic "homage" to male authority; Sharon McKern asserts, half-seriously, that a culture that "all but guarantees eccentricity as a feminine pre-rogative" allows ladies to do pretty much as they please.[11]

Several versions of the Southern lady-heroine *are* competent, powerful, and self-reliant, at least in the domestic sphere, and elsewhere when re-quired. But being too fine to cope is not seen as a defect: if a lady should happen to be submissive or dependent, or helpless, or overwhelmed, she does not automatically forfeit her positive evaluation. Recall that sub-missive and dependent men teeter on the edge of foolishness. Women to whom bad things happen, however, get to be victims. In that respect, at least, the range of social types open to white Southern females has been less constricting than the menu available to white Southern males.

A lady can be admired as heroic or victimized even if she has abdicated any claim to power, or exerts it only in a limited sphere. But a proper, conventional villain, to be *feared*, almost must be conventionally power-ful, which is why the most frequent form of villainy among upper-class Southern females has been based on *domestic* power. Just as the lady-heroine can be powerful in her own feminine sphere, so the lady-villain can be powerful in hers, and we encounter her as the castrating bitch figure in the works of some of the South's more recherché writers (Tennessee Williams comes to mind, of course). She turns husbands and sons into homosexuals, or sadomasochists, or impotent alcoholics, or (as in the case of Victor Jory, in *The Fugitive Kind*) all three.[12] Some have gone so far as to argue that the sexual division of labor traditional in the upper-class South in fact produced a "covert matriarchy," presided over by fierce "Norns" whose sons often turned out to be "stale gentle lisping bachelors with an obsession for antiques."[13] Unless, of course, they es-caped to the woods with the hunting band, as men are always wont to do in matriarchal societies.

This sort of psycho-sexual villainy may be pretty tame stuff, but until quite recently more conventional villainy has been a career largely closed to Southern ladies. Even in the period antislavery literature, cruel slave mistresses are much harder to find than cruel masters. Only in the his-torical fiction of our more enlightened time have the dramatic pos-sibilities of women with whips finally been realized.[14] Now, too, prime-time soap operas like "Dallas" and "Flamingo Road" have begun to portray

Southern upper-class women, like their menfolk, as characterized "by venality, conspicuous consumption, perverse familism, and manifest evil."[15] You've come a long way, baby.

When we turn to the *comic* lady (most commonly, a comic belle), again we find a range of sub-types, differing in competence: she can be anything from an utterly helpless airhead to a calculating, manipulative gold-digger. Either way, she evokes foolish behavior in men who ought to know better. The scatterbrained belle was a stock character in many old movies: run her on, listen to her talk, laugh, run her off. The Southern gold-digger was described by Helen Brown Norden, who claimed to know the type in New York: "Though outwardly all froth and fragility, she is really welded of indestructible steel. . . . When [she] surrenders her virtue, it is generally for a sound, practical reason like matrimony, her name in lights on Broadway, or a block of U.S. Steel." Miss Norden, the author of "Latins are Lousy Lovers," wrote somewhat resentfully that "Men love to make [Southern women] gifts because they are so charming when they receive them—just like children, all bubbling with excitement and affection."[16] This was written in the 1940s, but the same character can be found any Saturday night on "Hee-Haw," speaking of "my daddy, the Colonel."

I believe we are observing here at least the beginnings of an exception to the rule that Southern regional social types are similarly perceived North and South. Marshall Frady has argued, not at all gallantly, that "Southern women, on the whole, are a peculiar coy wine that does not travel well beyond its own indulgent clime. Northerners tend to find them faintly grotesque."[17] I doubt that Frady knows a cross-section of Northerners, but certainly there are non-Southern circles where women whom Southerners would regard as perfectly plausible and admirable specimens of femininity evoke amusement or scorn, in women and even some men.

In part, this is just that ol' debbil, Yankee ethnocentrism, which persists in misunderstanding Southern manners. (We will return to that subject in the next chapter.) Still, Southerners know what non-Southerners are talking about when they make fun of Southern belles. Some Southerners have even done it themselves on occasion. Like the gentleman, the belle is set up for ridicule, or at least for indulgent teasing, by her own pretensions. It takes real aplomb to pull off the role successfully before a skeptical audience. And there are many skeptics: our age is not a good one for old-fashioned heroes, or heroines.

Moving down the social ladder from the lady, we encounter a bewildering variety of female social types, a profusion and confusion that may have something to do with the fact that women of the white Southern lower classes did not figure prominently in the antebellum plantation myth. We have seen that Daniel Hundley, for instance, had a great deal to say about Southern men of all social classes; he and others certainly had much to say about Southern ladies, too. But the women attached to the yeomen, bullies, and trash of his sketch are mute, background figures. He complained about their snuff-dipping, and allowed that some of the young ones were uncommonly good-looking, but otherwise he was silent. Other observers, friendly or hostile, did little better.

As a result, our social typology for white Southern women who are not ladies is very largely a twentieth-century construction. Let us apply our apparatus of hero, villain, fool, and victim to the popular culture of this century and see what we come up with.

There seems to be no single, dominant heroine type in these social strata; there is no female yeoman, no working-class lady. Rather, there are several competing and to some extent mutually exclusive types, each with its own adherents and admirers.

Corresponding to the good old boy, and often found in his company, is the good old girl. She has the spunk, charm, and independence of Scarlett without her social aspirations. Perhaps the best description is from *People* magazine, describing the search that led to the casting of Catherine Bach as Daisy Duke, in "The Dukes of Hazzard," a search for "a tomboy who could drive a car and outshoot a man . . . the kind of girl who could also blow you away when she put on a pink cotton dress."[18] She is usually young, but an older version is not unknown: she may look something like the character Flo, in the television sitcom "Alice."

The good old girl has been around at least since World War II, in such third-rate novels as William Bradford Huie's *Revolt of Mamie Stover* where, as I recall, she was a working girl with a heart of gold. Lately this hell-raising, good-timing creature has begun to appear more and more in country music, drinking the boys under the table, or trying to. She has also become a staple in good old boy novels and movies, especially in sports epics like *Semi-Tough* and *North Dallas Forty*. Her status is roughly equivalent to that of the sidekick. Daisy Duke is unusual in being blood-kin to the good old boys: more often the good old girl is the hero's girlfriend or the sidekick's or both, one at a time or simultaneously.

Playboy magazine, after some unsuccessful experiments with the belle, seems to have settled on the good old girl type as its favored presentation of Southern women.[19] Miss April 1975, for example, was reportedly kicked out of stewardess school for being too rowdy, and (like Scarlett) enjoyed pistol shooting, with a special fondness for .45s and .357 magnums. Miss January 1982 was one of the last cut from the Dallas Cowboy cheerleaders, liked to buy fried chicken and eat it under the stars in the middle of empty football fields, and did not indicate a favorite book. You get the idea.

As these examples indicate, there is a racy aspect to the good old girl that may make her an unsuitable model for the average member of the Methodist Youth Fellowship. But a competing, and an older, type of blue-collar heroine may have broader appeal. Her roots are in the nineteenth-century farm wife, and we can call her simply the *good woman*.[20] We can think of her as an alternative to the good old girl; also, perhaps, as what the good old girl becomes when she marries and settles down.

Ruth Banes has written extensively about this type, newly revitalized and popularized in the songs and the personae of a number of female country-music stars. She is personified by Loretta Lynn, the strong, independent, ultra-competent coal-miner's daughter from Butcher Hollow, Kentucky.[21] Michael Hicks has described her: "The Good Woman should appear competent, wholesome, patient, but have a wild streak that's hidden most of the time." She has the "ability to bake pies, raise three children, and keep the house clean while working, singing, being a great lover, and saving coupons for the grocery store. The Good Woman is a goal for all lesser women to aspire to." Hicks adds that she should have a "country" name: "Loretta, Tammy, Dolly, Emmy Lou, or anything else besides Angelique."[22] (Actually, I see nothing wrong with Angelique, but Babs or Muffy would be out of the question.)

Every good old girl needs a hobby. This one collects stock-car racers. Valerie Perrine, with Jeff Bridges, in *The Last American Hero*. (Museum of Modern Art Film Stills Archive; 20th Century-Fox.)

Gidget goes union. Sally Fields as *Norma Rae* is a working-class heroine in the WPA tradition. (Museum of Modern Art Film Stills Archive; 20th Century-Fox.)

Unlike the lady, the good woman never even *pretends* to be helpless, and she deals with her man on terms of equality.[23] In this, she is also unlike an older country-music type, still found occasionally: the angel (not to be confused with the honkeytonk angel), a heroine so longsuffering that she verges on being a victim.[24] Sometimes the angel is the mama whose son winds up in prison despite her concerns and her prayers; more often, she is a "good-hearted woman in love with a good-timin' man."[25] Not surprisingly, perhaps, the angel appears most frequently in songs by male singers (like Conway Twitty's "How Much More Can She stand?"), but she is not wholly a male creation. If Loretta Lynn personifies the good woman, perhaps Tammy Wynette is the closest thing country music offers these days to an angel.[26] Miss Wynette, of course, sang "Stand By Your Man," the largest-selling country-music single ever recorded by a woman.

In the mythic South, women are victimized in many ways, and the WPA tradition I mentioned earlier offers countless examples of economic victims. At least as common and probably more compelling are women abandoned, neglected, or otherwise made miserable by their men, and country music is the place to go for examples of this sort.[27] In the banal myth of the straying husband, the villain is usually not the man (who gets away with the claim that he cannot help it), but rather the temptress, the Other Woman. Far and away, the most common form of villainy among working-class females—in country music, virtually the only form of it—is homewrecking.

True, it wasn't God who made honkytonk angels (and the song with that title broke new ground by presenting *them* as victims). Wherever they came from, though, they have usually been portrayed as bad figures, and powerful ones. These predators have the power to victimize men, and thereby to victimize other women, by taking their men more or less at will. Country songs with this message are also apt to be by male singers, but a number of female singers have gone along with it. In "Jolene," for instance, Dolly Parton sings to the other woman: "Please don't take him just because you can."

Recent years have seen some interesting new developments on this rather shopworn theme. For example, some songs have begun implicitly

Country music offers a paradigm of essences.

Loretta Lynn is not only a good woman, she is *the* good woman. (Peter Nash of Nashville.)

Hank Williams, the doomed hero-victim, with the longsuffering Miss Audrey. (John Edwards Memorial Collection, University of North Carolina, Chapel Hill.)

Hillbilly fools: Arthur Smith and the Dixie Liners cut up as white-face minstrels. (John Edwards Memorial Collection, University of North Carolina, Chapel Hill.)

Minnie Pearl is a character *sui generis*, but began as a hillbilly gal. (Minnie Pearl.)

to reject the double standard that underlies all of this. More are now written from the point of view of the Other Woman, and they present her in the same light as the man, a victim of uncontrollable passion. A few have even presented her as a good old girl, who just wants to have fun. Equally novel is a genre typified by a song called "You Ain't Woman Enough (To Take My Man)," written and recorded by Loretta Lynn. This song shows what happens when the temptress runs into a good woman instead of a doomed angel, and it rivals for drama anything that professional wrestling has to offer.[28]

But the point, again, is that women who are denied or who have foregone conventional sorts of power cannot be persuasive villains except in the spheres where they *do* have power. Like their upper-class sisters, working-class female villains have operated for the most part in the domestic theater. Only recently, and still rarely, has popular culture produced anything like a female version of the redneck villain, someone who threatens bodily harm, and even when she does appear, the redneck mama is usually a girlfriend, a camp follower. Sometimes she is literally a hanger-on, found on the back of a Harley-Davidson. She is not independently evil, as a rule: she just keeps bad company. At worst, she eggs them on.

But if the redneck villainess is essentially passive and dependent, except when luring men to destruction, that is certainly not the case for the comic lower-class female types: the hillbilly gal, the hillbilly wife, and the granny. Indeed, one funny thing about them is that they *are* competent, while their menfolk are lazy, inept, or both. If work is done, the women do it: the men are off hunting or fleeing from revenuers or reclining somewhere in communion with their jug and their dogs. This sex-role reversal is even institutionalized in Dogpatch's Sadie Hawkins Day. Even in the symbolically crucial business of gun-play, the women are probably as good as the men (recall Snuffy Smith's wife, Weezy). Much of this is ripe for Freudian analysis, but that alluring, Celtic mistress of the muck, Moonbeam McSwine, deserves special attention.

It certainly is no accident that both the redneck woman and the hillbilly gal are types with obvious components of sexuality. The redneck woman's

Tennessee Williams's characters are usually too bizarre to categorize, but in *Baby Doll* Carroll Baker carried the passive temptress to extremes condemned by the Legion of Decency. (Museum of Modern Art Film Stills Archive; United Artists.)

Li'l Abner often illustrates general themes with startling clarity. Here Daisy Mae rescues her helpless man from the irresistible Stupefyin' Jones in the movie adaptation of the stage play based on Al Capp's comic strip. (Museum of Modern Art Film Stills Archive; Paramount Pictures.)

is insistent and predatory: as Tony Joe White sings it, "Redneck women, they got that four-wheel drive," and that image flourishes in a genre of paperback subliterature with titles like *Swamp Hoyden* and *Backwoods Hussy*.[29] The hillbilly gal, on the other hand, offers something more easy-going and casual, suitable for family viewing, and available for it every week on "Hee Haw." Either way, these low-down, lower-class types stand in conspicuous contrast to the lady, who, if not sexless or repressed, is at least lacking in spontaneity. Even the belle is only a flirt, or tease.

The reason for this contrast is plain enough, and it brings us back full circle to the antebellum sources of the South's social typology. Positive lower-class types, like those of the good old boy and the good woman, seem to have originated largely among those being typed, in their self-images and their evaluations of their friends and neighbors. But the derogatory types, rednecks and hillbillies and their womenfolk, were originally upper-class constructions. As such, they share features with the stereotypes imposed on downtrodden "peasant" populations everywhere in the world. Promiscuous women; lazy, violent, and irresponsible men; dirtiness and stupidity all around—all of these go to make up what is known in the jargon of psychoanalytic social psychology as an "id" stereotype.

The idea is that members of the group doing the stereotyping project their unacceptable impulses onto the group being stereotyped, and can then deny that they have those impulses.[30] Antebellum ladies and gentlemen could feel even more genteel—that is, less inclined to dirtiness, laziness, irresponsibility, promiscuity, and so forth—if they could construct social types that *were* that way, and impose those types on their social inferiors—not only their black slaves, but their white neighbors as well.

They succeeded all too well, producing an array of types that achieved currency and notoriety outside the South, indeed around the world. The way they thought of Southern society became the way non-Southerners thought of it, and to a great extent it remains that today, a century after the quality and their society went down to dust. That they could impose and export their myth is powerful testimony to their cultural dominance. (Of course, these images provided some useful psychic services for non-

Southerners, too.) But the social typology that Daniel Hundley and his peers created never was an accurate description of their people, and it is even less adequate today. Let us examine some of its problems and inadequacies, and we will have to speculate about why, despite them, it has proven so durable.

Chapter Five

Butch and Wendy

The typology that I have outlined and filled in, I believe, pretty well exhausts the ways that white Southerners are presented in American popular culture, including those media intended primarily for Southern consumption. We have heroes, villains, fools, and victims; patrician and plebeian. The female types are sorted by age, and are in other ways more complicated than the male, but the general scheme is the same. Most of the types (all of the disreputable ones) were well-established before the Civil War, invented, I argued, by the antebellum Southern gentry and their Northern adversaries for purposes of their own.

With somewhat less conviction, I have also argued that these types largely define the terms in which twentieth-century Americans (Southerners included) think about white Southerners, *as Southerners*. Let me rephrase that, to be perfectly clear: When people think about white Southerners—not just about American folks who happen to be from the South—their thinking begins with these categories.

Finally, with some trepidation and little evidence aside from looking around me, I have suggested that these types do in fact correspond roughly to clusters of real people, some of them to the manner born, others *working* at it, with or without being aware of what they are doing.

But the typology does not even pretend to describe a great many people who live in the South. Who is omitted? First of all, black Southerners (and for that matter unassimilated members of all minority ethnic groups) are not here: twenty percent or so of the South's population. Neither are most migrants from the non-South: another twenty percent. Some migrants have been assimilated, and more of their children will be, but several sorts of migrants to the South are in the process of becoming social types in their own right (probably a good thing, too, since all there is to work with historically is the carpetbagger). No, this typology applies only to native white Southerners, not a great many more than half of the South's population today—and not all of them. The most numerous omission from this typology is the white middle class.

Look around you. There are not enough Yankee migrants to fill all of the South's new condominiums and real-estate developments. Who populates the South's fern bars? Would Daniel Hundley recognize them? Look in *Southern Living*. Who are these men standing around self-consciously in their backyards, wearing green blazers, eating hors d'oeuvres, and looking as if they would rather be inside watching the Redskins–Cowboys game?

None of the Southern social types we have examined is a solidly middle-class figure. This is an egregious blind-spot, a vacuum in our popular vocabulary for discussing, or even thinking about, the present-day South.

It is tempting to attribute this omission to the fact that there was not much of a Southern middle class to *be* typed when this typology came into being in the antebellum period. But that is itself stereotypical thinking; there were many middle-class Southerners even then, and Daniel Hundley examined them.[1] He wrote in *Social Relations in Our Southern States* that the South's middle class was "very numerous, very useful, and . . . in many respects very worthy." It included "farmers, [some] planters, traders, storekeepers, artisans, mechanics, a few manufacturers, a goodly number of country school-teachers, and a host of half-fledged country lawyers and doctors, parsons, and the like."

But he had the same problem we do today: there were no middle-class *social types* for him to describe.[2] He complained because Northerners saw the white South as a simple two-class structure of gentry and lower class. But he showed, in effect, that most Southerners saw things the same way. Middle-class Southern men, by his account, refused to recognize that they were not gentlemen. They persisted in trying to act like gentlemen, insisted on being treated like gentlemen, no doubt sustained each other in this impersonation. (Hundley wished they would cut it out. Some people, he said, looked down on the middle class, but *he* thought no less of men who lacked the birth, manners, and education of gentlemen. I fear his examination of the middle class speaks less to his acuity as a social observer than to the fact that he was something of a snob.)

Hundley's treatment reflected the absence of middle-class social types in a back-handed way. He devoted a chapter apiece to upper-class heroes, villains, and fools, and another three chapters to their lower-class counterparts. But he treated the middle class the same way he treated blacks: he lumped them all together in one chapter—not heroic, villainous, or even foolish, just "very numerous, very useful, and . . . in many respects very worthy." Small wonder that the middle class preferred to wear the garments of the gentry, to the chagrin of those like Hundley who felt they had no right to them. Hundley was quite right that the Southern class structure was complicated and many-tiered, but Northerners and most Southerners alike contrived to ignore that fact.

What has changed since Hundley's time? Well, the Southern middle class is certainly more numerous, probably more useful, and maybe even more worthy than ever.[3] Half of the South's labor force is now in white-collar occupations; half of the white-collar workers, a quarter of all Southern workers, are in managerial and professional jobs. Clearly our social typology is even less adequate now than it was in 1860.

Witness the difficulty the media had with Jimmy Carter and his relatives. Billy appeared to be no problem: he was obviously a good old boy of an utterly familiar sort. And Miz Lillian was a lady, no doubt about that. But what did that make their son and brother, the president? Was he a good old boy like Billy? Or his mother's son, a gentleman? Or something else altogether? It was all very confusing. "There is something about Jimmy Carter which makes him opaque to me," a *New Yorker* correspondent wrote. Her Southern friends, she noted, did not have that problem, but she just could not pigeonhole the man.

People can hardly help seeing the Southern middle class, but they cannot talk about it easily in the shorthand of social types. The old regional labels are not quite *right*, but the standard American labels do not do justice to its *Southerness*.

I have a friend who writes for *Southern Living*. He tells me that some of his colleagues have a mental image of the people they are writing for. Butch and Wendy live with their two children, Bubba and Michelle, in a subdivision house on a sloping lot with poor drainage—and so forth. Here we have the makings of some social types, coming into being in the classic way: because they are useful. There are Butches and Wendys all over the South today. But as labels for the social types they are still the private property of some writers for *Southern Living*.

Why have middle-class Southern social types been so slow to emerge? Can it be that there is no reason to think of them apart from other middle-class Americans—that middle-class Southerners are not usefully thought of as "Southern?" I do not believe that, and Butch and Wendy do not believe it either. *Most* Americans, Southern and non-Southern, do not believe it, and they are right.[4] There are large, persistent regional differences in this country, even among middle-class urban and suburban people.[5]

It is not that the media have brainwashed us into retaining the old types, either. There is no Yankee plot to misrepresent the South by denying the existence of a middle class. The media are just trying to sell advertising, and (as Dr. Johnson said) one is seldom more innocently engaged than when trying to make money. People do not willfully believe false things about the South. We can give almost everybody credit for good intentions, or at least indifference.

This is not to say, however, that regional stereotypes do not serve important social and psychological functions for those who hold them. If Americans have been willing to make do with the hand-me-downs of the plantation myth despite its diminishing *cognitive* usefulness (its diminishing utility, that is, as summary description of the Southern reality), these antebellum types must have something else to offer Southerners and non-Southerners alike.

For almost everyone, no doubt, the derogatory lower-class types, redneck villains and comic hillbillies, serve the same "mudsill" function as they did when some ladies and gentlemen of the antebellum South found that thinking in terms of these types allowed them to believe comforting things about themselves. "AntiSouthernism," C. Vann Woodward has written,

is the antiAmericanism of the North. It performs many of the rationalizations and defenses that antiAmericanism performs for Europeans. It channels and releases many of the same sort of anxieties, fears, resentments, flatters many of the same vanities, fosters moral and cultural snobberies and hypocrisies, releases similar aggressions and resentments.[6]

Of course, these types play a part not only in relations between North and South, but also in social-class relations within the South. There is no need to belabor the point, but Northerners are not the only modern Americans who speak disparagingly about rednecks and hillbillies.

In addition, these types have considerable entertainment value, as do the derogatory upper-class types. For obvious reasons, avarice, lust, sadism, buffoonery, and general dissipation in high places have always and everywhere had box office appeal for the great many who are not themselves in high places. In addition, the "Black Legend" of the antebellum slavocracy was *politically* useful, in the 1960s no less than in the 1860s, and I suggested that we may now be seeing the emergence of something similar to deal with the Sunbelt plutocracy, the Ted Turners and J. R. Ewings.

The continuing popularity of the positively evaluated types may take a little more explaining. Why do some non-Southerners persist in believing good things—the same old good things—about white Southerners? Why do some middle-class Southerners use these seemingly obsolete types to classify themselves and their middle-class friends? Why, that is, do many Americans of all regions continue to think of Southerners with white-collar jobs, cable television, and Cuisinarts as ladies and gentlemen, on the one hand, or as good old boys and good women, on the other?

Part of the explanation surely lies in the fact that these types, too, are entertaining. They present a stimulating counterpoint to the facts of middle-class life, North or South. Those facts are not very interesting. They never have been, anywhere. Like the solid middle-class citizens of Hundley's time who aspired to the dash and courtliness and honor of the quality, Butch and Wendy are not heroic, they are not villainous, they are not victimized in any serious way—they are not even very funny. Some have speculated that the Southern lady and gentleman, "like beauty queens in this century, [have] provided relief from the dogma and reality of leveling democracy."[7] (Those beauty queens themselves, of course, have often been Southern belles.)

Many non-Southerners seem to have tired of the mythic gentry of the South these days, or at least have come to doubt their heroic *bona fides* in contexts other than historical. (And beauty queens are not what they used to be, either). But the Southern lady and gentleman still serve those who believe in them in much the same way the monarchy now serves Great Britain, providing a glamorous image of elegance and grace, without the annoyance of real authority.

And the working-class figures, the good old boy and his various kinds of womenfolk—their laid-back insouciance and *joie de vivre* also provide a refreshing contrast to buttoned-down white-collar ordinariness. As Jack Temple Kirby sees it, "the yearning of the late '60s Counterculture for bucolic simplicity somehow attached itself to the rural South." What had previously identified the redneck killers of Captain America—country music, pickup trucks, Levis, even chewing tobacco—ironically came to stand for a countercultural style, one briefly identified with the Carter White House (and, not incidentally, one that offered a standing reproach to the "best and brightest" whose up-tight, Ivy League, cost-effective ways had run out of steam in the Southeast Asian jungles).[8]

As Kirby observes, all of the Southern types, upper-class or lower, are *pre-modern* types. Most are "impractical, improvident, and not fond of work." At one time (and, in some quarters, still) that was not a good way to be; so "Southerners' different values and styles helped Yankees see themselves as proper, tolerant, industrious, productive—i.e., normal and American." Perhaps increasingly (and, in some quarters, always) "impractical, improvident, and not fond of work" is a *good* way to be, so these romantic, non-bourgeois types have been admired and envied, too.

The residual appeal of the lady and gentleman, the emergent popularity of the Southern plain folk, and the new facts of Southern middle-class life have given Butch and Wendy and their friends a heady new freedom. No one is imposing any particular types on them: there are no specifically Southern middle-class social types to impose. So they are free to choose, and the range of choice is wider than ever. They can take their models from the basic steak-and-potatoes (or quiche-and-salad) American menu, and believe themselves to be more or less indistinguishable from other middle-class Americans. Or, like the Southern middle class of Hundley's day, they can elect to be Southern ladies and gentlemen, and garner what remains of the attendant honor and esteem. Or, lately, they can choose to be good old boys and girls, peppering their speech with the "Southern provincialisms and Africanisms" that Hundley disliked, buying Emmy Lou Harris tapes for the car stereo, and whooping it up at college football games. Indeed, if they want, they can be yuppies and gentry and yeomen on alternate days, or even somehow all three simultaneously. The playing out of these social types is not always entirely unstudied, nor is it always convincing, but it is certainly a phenomenon that is there to be observed.

Do these types have a future? Certainly they will survive as summary statements about groups of living people where their lineage is longest and their accuracy greatest, among the South's farm population and its blue-collar city cousins, on the one hand, and among what is left of the old-line Southern upper class, on the other. But what is to become of them among the Southern middle class, that rapidly growing near-majority of the South's population? What will Butch and Wendy make of them?

As Junior Samples used to say, "I don't know nothin', but I *suspect* a lot of things." Let us take a look at some of the factors that I suspect will determine the answers to those questions.

Why are the gentleman-hero and the lady-heroine (especially in the form of the belle) harder to take seriously these days? For many Americans, even some Southerners, these types have a tendency to slide over into their comic forms. Why is that?

I believe that the problem lies in their manners. All social types, of course, are embodied in "manners," styles, of some sort. But the Southern lady and gentleman are defined in large part by their *good* manners, in the conventional "yes, ma'am" sense. So long as they interact mostly with other Southerners, this presents no difficulties. Southerners understand that this sort of behavior means only that those who display it have had proper raising, or have made up for the lack of it. It says very little about their character or their attitudes toward the people they are interacting with. But non-Southerners often misunderstand.

The misunderstanding works both ways, of course. Northerners have manners of their own. Southerners, ethnocentrically, are likely to see them as *bad*, although by and large they are too polite to say so. Northerners, of course, prefer to think of themselves as direct, straightforward, no-nonsense, at least as compared to Southerners, whose behavior they tend to find amusing if sincere, hypocritical or calculating if not.

At best, perhaps, outsiders find Southerners hard to figure. Choong Soon Kim, for example, author of *An Asian Anthropologist in the South,* writes that Southerners "tend to be very diplomatic when they speak. They avoid any straightforward expressions if possible."[9] He finds Southerners, in a word, inscrutable.

Here, in manners, is one great remaining regional difference, with great potential for mutual incomprehension, possibly tragic, but often funny. For example, Florence King has told about her trials as a woman with Southern manners in New York:

> Southern women flirt so automatically that half the time they don't even realize they are doing it. . . . Southern men know the difference [between social flirtation and the real thing]; Northern men do not (understandably, since Northern women, especially New Yorkers, simply don't carry on in this fashion). When you rattle off a standard Southern thank-you—"Oh, you're just so nice, I don't know what I'd *do* without you!" the Northern man *believes you!* He believes you so much that he follows you home.[10]

As we saw in the last chapter, some Northern women, at least, find it hard to believe that Southern women do not know what they are doing.

Most Southerners who have spent time outside the South could tell similar stories. Here are a few more, from a writer in the *Texas Observer:*

> I was once severely criticized by a liberal New York lawyer for apologizing to a waitress. "Why are you so condescending?" he demanded.
>
> When I rose to be introduced to a woman in her late sixties, I was chastised for excessive formality.
>
> Dropping into one of my oldest habits, I said "Yes, ma'am" to a friend's mother, causing her to shriek with laughter. "Ma'am!" she howled. "Isn't that cute? *My God!*"[11]

Northern migrants to the South have their problems, too. One Northern woman complained to *U.S. News and World Report* that her "nosy" Southern neighbor had once asked her when her traveling husband was coming home. Southern manners, of course, dictate that you inquire about your acquaintances' kinfolk: the neighbor quite possibly had no interest at all in the answer.[12]

Here is a Florida businesswoman (she would want it on the record that she was raised in Charleston) on the difference between Northern and Southern women: "I think it is a softness that Southern women have that Yankees don't have, at least the Yankees I know—*some* of the Yankees I know." And listen to a retired Tampa schoolteacher try to answer the question "Are Northern women domineering?" without giving offense: "I would say more so than Southern women, but they're not really." She knows one Northern woman who is not domineering. "But she's very capable. She really is capable. And she really is domineering in a way, but I mean she's genteel. She's not pushy. Well, she is pushy in a way, because she's got to get her way."[13]

These mutual misunderstandings extend even to ideas about what a conversation is. Conversation in New York, Roy Reed has written, is "hurled stones"; in the South, it is "moonshine passed slowly to all who care to lift the bottle."[14] Eudora Welty's character, Miss Edna Earle Ponder, feared that her dimwitted Uncle Daniel would run into some guest at her hotel who "would break in on a story with a set of questions, and wind it up with a list of what Uncle Daniel's faults were: some Yankee."[15]

Going on with these stories all day would be a very Southern way to go about this, but surely these are enough to make my point. A society that puts Southerners in frequent contact with non-Southerners calls Southern manners into question more often and in more ways than one where Southerners are dealing almost exclusively with one another. This eats away at the social types that live and die by their manners. They become self-conscious and sometimes uncomfortable. Nobody enjoys being suspect, or unintentionally amusing.

Nevertheless, among ourselves, these types have their exemplars, their devotees, and their rewards. I believe this is particularly so for women. The Southern lady is in much less danger than the Southern gentleman of becoming merely a period piece trotted out for Chamber of Commerce events and historical dramas. Marshall Frady has even argued that "*all*

Southern women answer and ravenously aspire" to "a manner of ladyhood—a feminine gentility."[16]

When he said "all," of course, he was overstating, which is almost customary in these matters. (He might be well-advised to listen to Roy Blount, Jr.: "I cannot speak with authority—not with authority as it is known in the South—about Southern women. I am acquainted with no more than two-thirds of them, and several of those I haven't seen in some time."[17]) Discounting Frady's overstatement, though, he offered some valuable observations: for example, that ladyhood is "an improbably democratic order, encompassing not only afternoon teas in antebellum mansions but all the gatherings of the women's missionary circles of the Calvary Baptist Churches amid gladioli and antimacassars." As a political reporter, Frady was particularly sensitive to political ladies. "All over the South now," he observed,

> there can be found the wives of prospering political figures, somewhat metallic and heatless women whose origins were the slatternly grease-sizzling outskirts of little slumping towns and who, as their husbands' fortunes rose, instinctively and systematically began to acquire tastes for glass figurines and enormous billowy hats and rather depthless precise nature paintings, along with an air of twinkling blitheness, and thereby reconstituted themselves, for all practical purposes, as Southern ladies.[18]

Frady acknowledged the presence of "a different population of [Southern] women—mostly found in those instant outer suburbs of life-scale dollhouses of imitation Tudor and Georgian and Seville and Fontainebleau, a surrealistic frontier out in the jack pines and broom sage and red dirt," women who "to a large degree are indistinguishable from housewives in Des Moines or Omaha or Cincinnati." At the same time, he saw "in the measureless apartment warrens of cities like Atlanta an enormous host of young single girls," come from the small towns of the Southern outback to "cluster in fours in the downtown pubs and steakhouses during lunchtime"—"Melanie Wilkeses [transmuted] into a generation of airline stewardesses." But, with these few million exceptions, Frady insisted that the Southern lady remains a compelling ideal for "all" Southern women.[19]

Be that as it may (and it still smacks of overstatement), some of Frady's exceptions are probably not exceptions after all. Who could possibly be more "New South" than the general manager of an imported automobile business in Tampa? Listen to Vivian Reeves, of Reeves Import Autos: "I can only speak for myself," she says, "but I have always felt that I could say whatever I wanted to say as long as it was in a lady-like fashion."[20] Only speaking for herself is, of course, a very lady-like way to go about it.

Clearly, in considerable numbers, and for better or for worse, the Southern lady has made the transition from plantation society to the urban, industrial society that the South is now. She has made that transition both as ideal and reality—as a social type. She is no longer the *only* ideal, and some of her characteristics have changed to make her compatible with, for example, selling foreign cars, but she is alive and well and visible to all those with eyes to see.

Her consort, the gentleman, seems a more sickly character these days. We saw that he still has some vitality in historical drama and fiction, but I believe that he has lost some of his appeal as a living ideal for white Southern men. In particular, I suspect that middle-class males find the idea of being gentlemen a good deal less attractive than their womenfolk find the idea of being ladies.

The gentleman has the same problems as the lady; his manners, too, are often suspect or amusing. In addition, we heard from Florence King that the gentleman's style is sometimes seen to verge on *fussiness*, which makes him vulnerable to a particularly distressing form of misunderstanding. "Every Southern man," she writes (not indicating how many she knows, or how lately she has seen them),

> harbors a certain resentful fear of the Southern-gentleman image. It smacks of the drawing room and the dancing master; it suggests that he hovers in attendance upon women (which he most certainly does); that he is over-civilized, over-housebroken, even foppish. One part of him wants to squire the ladies in style, and another part of him wants to get away from them and take to the woods.[21]

Perhaps this has always been true, if it is true at all. What has certainly changed is that the social rewards for playing the gentleman have diminished. At the same time, a more intrinsically enjoyable alternative has emerged, in the person of the good old boy, who indeed often does get away from the ladies and take to the woods.

Why does this character appeal to today's middle-class Southern males more than the yeoman, his ancestor, did to yesterday's? Daniel Hundley complained that the middle class of his day went around pretending to be more genteel than they actually were; he could not have imagined that someday their descendants would aspire to more down-home common-ness than they came by naturally.

In part, this may simply reflect a more general phenomenon of the 1960s, a decade in which many fashions—in clothing, music, and speech, for example—began to trickle up from near the bottom rather than down from the top of the social-class ladder. Why not social types, fashions in personal style, as well? Of course, it is not at all obvious why the more general inversion took place; and it is not clear yet (at least not to me) whether it was merely temporary or was part of a long-term pro-cess of cultural democratization. Perhaps the Southern-born journalist and social observer Tom Wolfe has had as much to say about this as any-one else: his discussion of *nostalgie de la boue,* "nostalgia for the mud," is very much to the point here.[22]

The fact that the red clay is only a couple of generations behind most middle-class Southerners suggests still another possible factor in the popularity of these essentially rural types. It could be that we are seeing an example of what has been called the "third generation" phenomenon, in which ethnic revival is found among third-generation Americans, chil-dren of parents who were at some pains to disown *their* parents' embar-rassing, "foreign" ways.[23]

Certainly, as I suggested earlier, one heritage of the sixties was a re-valuation of laid-back, "id" styles, which now appeal to a great many who are otherwise nothing like flower children. Having a good time emerged from the sixties as a respectable thing to be into, and for those who are into it the good old boy's spontaneity and high spirits compare favorably not only to Northern or middle-class banality but to upper-class restraint. Nobody ever said being a gentleman was *fun.*

More than that: The good old boy style is *fakey.* As a matter of honor, the true gentleman demands to be taken at his own estimation. In contrast, like the best basketball players (who are usually black, of course), the good old boy enjoys deception, evasion, and good moves. Consequently, it seems to me, he prefers to be *under*estimated, at least initially: it gives him room to maneuver. Roy Reed has written about something similar, discussing what he sees as a regional propensity for "indirection":

> If any one eccentricity nourishes the Southerner and gives him space to perform and struggle and fight, it is indirection. . . . No discussion, sermon or quarrel should be telescoped when it can be drawn out all afternoon with endless opportunity for dodging, feinting and keeping one's position obscured. . . . Indirection is not dishonesty. It is simply a matter of style.[24]

But it does explain why Lyndon Johnson said that whenever he heard someone say "I'm just a country boy," he checked to make sure his wallet was still there.

For whatever reasons, since the sixties the good old boy has been a popular type with middle-class Southern men, so much so that one well-placed observer implies that he has now become an almost exclusively middle-class figure.[25] I doubt that, frankly, but certainly the working-class original is no longer a great deal more numerous than what *Time* magazine identified as "the more polished subspecies of conscious good ole boys who abound in small-town country clubs."[26]

Butch (remember him?) is likely to be this sort of good old boy, at least a good deal of the time. But Wendy is probably still a lady, most of the time. The good old boy and the lady—sounds like the title of a country song, and it may well be. Certainly it has been the theme of several, which tend to view the combination as anomalous. I am suggesting, however, that, if we focus on style rather than actual social class, this sort of couple is easy to find in the small-town and suburban South.

It is not even unknown among the South's public figures. No one, so far as I know, has ever mistaken Governor Wallace of Alabama for a gentleman; I doubt that he has ever aspired to be one, or particularly respects those who are. Those who admire him would doubtless proclaim him a good old boy. But his late wife, Lurleen, said once that the figures she most admired in all of human history were (in her words) "those brave and gracious ladies of the South who fought such hardships and tried to hold things together back during the War between the States, and that dreadful period afterward."[27]

In the terms defined by the recent outpouring of research on Americans' sex-role stereotypes, the lady and the good old boy are the most "feminine" and "masculine," respectively, of the positive Southern social types. There is no androgyny here, and the combination can produce a household that liberal opinion must disapprove. A *New York Times* review of the Moe Bandy and Joe Stampley album "Just Good Ol' Boys," for example, observed that "If one paused and gave these songs serious thought, they might raise disturbing questions about marital morality."[28] (This ranks right up there for party-pooping sobriety with a *Times* article on "The Waltons," which remarked that "From a feminist viewpoint Olivia's decision to abandon her career as a singer is dreadful."[29])

Certainly these two social types are vastly different, but there is surprisingly little correspondence between their characteristics and what Americans apparently tend to see as feminine and masculine traits. A catalog of stereotypical sex differences compiled by a team of social psychologists in Massachusetts, for example, probably tells us more about the New England college students who supplied the list than about styles of masculinity and femininity in the South, Old or New.[30]

The Southern lady, for instance, may well be "tactful," "gentle," "talkative," and "aware of the feelings of others," although it is easy to think of individual exceptions who remain undeniably ladies. But do Southern ladies have "difficulty making decisions?" Surely it depends on the lady, and the decision. Do they "lack self-confidence?" Hardly, in my (admittedly limited) experience. And there are other respects in which Southern ladies are not reliably feminine, in the terms laid down by New England undergraduates.

Nor is the good old boy 100% "masculine," although certainly the real item has an element of machismo in his make-up and would not appreciate my saying so. He is "independent" and doesn't cry much. He probably is "sloppy," "loud," "rough," and "comfortable about being aggressive." He may well "[have] difficulty expressing tender feelings," and be "calm in a minor crisis" (or even a major one). But is he even usually taciturn, or "blunt?" Is he "objective?" (About what?) It is difficult to say whether someone is "easily able to separate feelings from ideas" if he seldom tries. Some good old boys are "skilled in business," but that is hardly a requirement; and one who is "fond of math and science" sounds almost like a contradiction in terms, although I have known Clemson graduates who are good old boys *despite* that. ("Old Earl, he's fond of math and science, but he's a good old boy.")

In part, I am simply repeating that although these social types tell us important things about the people they are applied to, they tell us only a *few* things. They specify sex, race, and the attitude of the speaker, and they tell us something increasingly imprecise about social class. Aside from that, what they tell us principally is something about manners.

These are, as Marshall Frady said, "improbably democratic" types, and very popular ones. They must accommodate themselves to a wide range of humanity. The lady has "good" manners; the good old boy has easygoing ones. Both kinds of manners can be learned, and neither tells us much about personality, character, or intelligence. Virtually all that the many *kinds* of ladies have in common are their manners, which together add up to a style, more or less internalized, and labeled as a social type: "lady."[31] Beyond that, it is foolish to generalize. The same is true of the good old boy, and indeed of virtually all of the types we have examined.

But even where people might be willing to generalize, the differences between the good old boy and lady are not always what most students of American gender stereotypes would predict. According to those same New England students, for example, expecting obedience is supposedly a masculine trait, and irresponsibility is a feminine prerogative. But here we have ladies with whims of iron and happy-go-lucky good old boys.

The explanation, of course, is that supposed gender differences are overlaid here on social-class differences: the lady was originally an upper-class type and the good old boy a working-class one. Since acting as if obedience is expected is part of an upper-class style and happy-go-luckiness is a positive trait only for working-class males (a happy-go-lucky gentleman is a fool), sometimes the women act as if they expect to be obeyed, and the men affect irresponsibility.

And, as we saw, sometimes they are husband and wife. Walker Percy has written about this sort of couple, and he really has their number. Here Lancelot Lamar talks about women like his wife:

> Did you know that the South and for all I know the entire U.S.A. is full of demonic women who, driven by as yet unnamed furies, are desperately restoring and preserving *places, buildings?* women married to fond indulgent easygoing somewhat lapsed men like me, who would as soon do one thing as another as long as they can go fishing, hunting, drink a bit, horse around, watch the Dolphins and Jack Nicklaus on TV. So here's this fellow like me who maybe had a moment of glory in his youth, in football, in Phi Beta Kappa, as Grand Dragon of his fraternity, and now is managing Auto-Lec or Quik-Stop and every night comes home to a museum such as not even George Washington slept in.[32]

The double irony is that Lance himself is of genteel Louisiana descent, while his wife is a former good old girl from Texas.

That is enough, perhaps too much, about this topic. I have dwelt on it because the good old boy and the lady (perhaps under other labels) seem to be the specifically *regional* types with the greatest appeal to the white Southern middle class, for the time being at least. An interesting question for social-type watchers is whether the middle-class adaptations of these types will continue to suffice, or whether distinctively middle-class Southern types will emerge—or, for that matter, whether Southern types will become something like the cowboy: well-known figures of historical interest, and objects of nostalgia.

I suspect my grandchildren will be able to answer that question. But if no living Southern types remain I doubt that anyone will be interested in the answer.

To close, let me ask a few other fifty-year questions, and venture a few predictions.

The lady and gentleman, heroic and villainous—what will become of them? They will certainly survive, at least as the cowboy survives. They will still be a presence in historical fiction and drama, where the sectional

conflict (more precisely, the conflict between the plantation and abolitionist myths of the Old South) has made the transition to the miniseries
format with little change other than hairstyle (although some of us feel
that Lesley-Ann Down is no Vivien Leigh).

Can these powerful upper-class types be recast in contemporary terms?
With the rise of the Sunbelt, will the up-scale Southern villain make a
come-back? Will he look like J. R. Ewing? Jesse Helms? Pat Robertson?

Can the gentleman-hero be rehabilitated? Can he overcome the "fussiness" Florence King complained about? He surely will not make it as
Ashley Wilkes; he will have to be something of a rogue, with the raffish pa-
nache of (say) Rhett Butler. Some Yankees have tried to paint Ted Turner
as a villain; can anything be done with him as a hero?

And poor Ashley. The way Leslie Howard played him, as Fred Chappell
has pointed out, he became something of "a polite prototype for the sexu-
ally injured southern males in later films" like those of Tennessee
Williams.[33] He and his fellow male victims, of whatever social class, have
their problems, not just as human beings but as social types, at least for
local consumption. But some women feel sorry for them, and so do some
sentimental young men, and some Yankee artists and journalists—
enough of an audience, taken together, to ensure the type's survival until
better times.

The *comic* types will survive, too, both gentry and poor-white. Americans are unlikely to find other ethnic fools as satisfactory or defenseless
as the hillbilly and his womenfolk. And since even Dogpatch has its local
notables, the Colonel's future is also secure (and he needs a comic belle of
a daughter to call him daddy). He makes a good ineffectual bad guy, too,
as Boss Hogg will demonstrate in syndicated reruns for decades.

The cultural politics of those survivals are worth pondering, and so are
those of the redneck villain, who also seems to have carved out a durable
place for himself. The principal question I am looking to answer these
days is not whether we will see more villainous redneck women in the
future (we will), but what they will look like. Will they break out of their
role as camp-followers and become scary in their own right?

Will the bull market in working-class heroes last? The good old boy, like

Rhett Butler and Ashley Wilkes define contrasting styles of the Southern gentleman and illustrate, respectively, the promise and the problems inherent in the type. (Museum of Modern Art Film Stills Archive; Metro-Goldwyn-Mayer.)

Middle-class males may prefer to skip the whole thing and be good old boys instead. Here, four take to the woods, in *Deliverance*. (Museum of Modern Art Film Stills Archive; Warner Bros.)

his cousin the urban cowboy, seems to have worn out his welcome in some quarters. He will certainly survive where he started, among working-class Southerners, but will middle-class Southern males abandon him for yuppiehood or whatever comes after that?

Or will Southerners somehow assimilate national trends in social-typing and make them their own? They may. The hillbilly gals of "Hee Haw" now do aerobic dance routines, for example, and a recent song by Hank Williams, Jr., has him and his rowdy friends in his hot tub, drinking beer and waiting for the pig to cook.

And what of the lady? She has survived the loss of cheap domestic help and the dramatic increase in the size of the white middle class, and she still has surprising appeal to those Southern women with the means to emulate her. She has changed some, in a gradual, grudging, incremental way, but will she still be recognizable—will she still be even a coherent type—if present trends in family life and female employment continue?

Those changes probably already mean that female victims get less sympathy than they once did. At least in working-class circles, to judge from country music, there is a growing view that they should stand up and fight back. The working-class heroine seems to be in transition, from the long-suffering angel—to what? My guess is that the good woman will consolidate her grip on those women with no realistic aspirations to ladyhood. The good old girl will have her fans, but they are more likely to be men than women.

Will there ever be a unisex Southern type? I doubt it, but that may just be a failure of the imagination. (All I can come up with is something like a female good old boy—a revolting idea, although perhaps not impossible.) This is not to say that nationally advertised varieties will have no appeal in the South, only that it is hard to imagine a type that would include both Southern women and Southern men, while excluding non-Southerners.

I am confident that stereotypically Southern social types will survive in the mass media, and not just in historical settings. I am a little less confident about their future in real life, but the media will help keep them alive there, too. (Recall the "feedback hillbilly" phenomenon.) When a writer, or a television producer, or a country musician wants for some reason to set his product in the South, or even to use Southern characters in a mixed setting, he will use identifiably Southern types.

Some people can wax indignant about this. Roy Blount, Jr., for instance, has pointed out that in many television situation comedies "you can calibrate how much of a bungler a character is by the strength of his Southern accent."[34] And Jack Temple Kirby gets annoyed because that wholesome television family "The Waltons" lost their Virginia accents as they went along. "What all this means," he wrote, "is that when Southerners achieve American norms of behavior, they cease being Southerners. Or conversely, to be Southern, popular culture characters must be eccentric, neurotic, lazy, bloodthirsty, past-worshipping, Jehovah-obsessed, or race-baiting—or a combination of all of the above or worse."[35]

Actually, it is not that bad: quaint or cute will do. But there is no question that television and other mass media portray Southerners as *different*—or they do not portray Southerners at all. But that is to be expected. If your characters are not identifiably Southern, why bother to use Southern characters?

Blacks were once caught in the same dilemma. The point of black characters was their blackness. If you were not portraying ghetto or rural Southern characters, why distract your (white) audience by using black actors? It was only when it became a duty to make a different point—that black folks were just like other Americans (maybe more so)—that we began to see normal, middle-class blacks on television programs and commercials. I do not see much of anybody besides Jack Kirby lobbying to make a similar point about white Southerners.

The reasons are obvious enough. In the first place, some of the types are admirable ones: people do not object to flattering stereotypes, even if they are distortions. In the second place, since Southerners use these types themselves (indeed, invented them) they can enjoy representations even of the unflattering ones, in the belief that they apply to *other* Southerners, not themselves.

One other consideration encourages me to believe that Southern social types will still be around to amuse and appall my grandchildren. I am not sure how to put this, so let me call one last time on a Southern humorist to do it for me, by indirection. Roy Blount, Jr., writes:

> If a Northern visitor makes it clear to Southerners that he thinks it would be typical of them to rustle up a big, piping hot meal of hushpuppies and blackstrap, Southerners will do that, even if they were planning to have just a little salad that night.
>
> Then the visitor will ask how to eat hushpuppies and blackstrap. . . . The strictly accurate answer is that nobody in his or her right mind eats these two things, together, in any way at all. But that isn't a sociable answer. So Southerners may say, "First you pour your plate full of the molasses, and then you crumble your hushpuppies up in it, and then you take the *back* of your spoon, and . . ." Southerners will say things like that just to see whether it is still true that Northerners will believe anything. About the South.[36]

"Southerners," Blount writes, "get a charge out of being typical."

Notes

Introduction

1. *Wall Street Journal*, 13 June 1985, 1.
2. Quoted in Greil Marcus, *Mystery Train: Images of America in Rock 'n' Roll Music* (New York: E. P. Dutton, 1975), 149.
3. Quoted in George Brown Tindall, *The Ethnic Southerners* (Baton Rouge: Louisiana State University Press, 1976), 43.
4. William Faulkner, *Absalom, Absalom!* (New York: Random House, 1936), 217.
5. Marshall Frady, quoted in Thomas L. Connelly and Barbara L. Bellows, *God and General Longstreet: The Lost Cause and the Southern Mind* (Baton Rouge: Louisiana State University Press, 1982), 138.
6. Historians' work on this topic has been usefully collected in Patrick Gerster and Nicholas Cords, eds., *Myth and Southern History*, 2 vols. (Chicago: Rand McNally, 1974). See especially George Tindall's "Mythology: A New Frontier in Southern History," reprinted there and in Tindall, *The Ethnic Southerners*. The work of literary scholars has not been so conveniently assembled, but much of it is cited here. (Two off-beat pieces not otherwise cited are Earl F. Bargainnier, "Tin Pan Alley and Dixie: The South in Popular Song," *Mississippi Quarterly* 30 [Fall 1977]: 527–64, and Peter A. Soderbergh, "The South in Juvenile Series Books, 1907–1917," *Mississippi Quarterly* 27 [Spring 1974]: 131–40.) As my bibliography makes clear, this topic has also concerned students of folklore and popular culture, as well as some social scientists.
7. F. N. Boney, "The American South," *Journal of Popular Culture* 10 (Summer 1976): 293.
8. C. Vann Woodward, "Southern Styles, Black and White," *Chapel Hill Weekly*, April 16, 1972.

9. Orrin E. Klapp, *Heroes, Villains, and Fools: The Changing American Character* (Englewood Cliffs, N.J.: Prentice-Hall, 1962).

10. Thomas L. Connelly, *The Marble Man: Robert E. Lee and His Image in American Society* (New York: Alfred A. Knopf, 1977).

11. Edgar T. Thompson, "Decency and the Good Old Boy Syndrome," *South Atlantic Quarterly* 83 (Autumn 1984): 434.

12. For an early essay that could help in sketching that typology—an essay now, I am sure, somewhat out-of-date—see E. Franklin Frazier, "Certain Aspects of Conflict in the Negro Family," *Social Forces* 10 (October 1931): 76–84.

Chapter One

1. Klapp, *Heroes, Villains, and Fools.*

2. This is the first of what will be many references to country music lyrics. I have not cited their sources in any formal way, since I do not believe that being treated solemnly is good for country music. Obviously, however, I believe it can be taken seriously. For a good discussion of why, see Charles F. Gritzner, "Country Music: A Reflection of Popular Culture," *Journal of Popular Culture* 11 (Spring 1978): 857–64.

3. "[A]s well look for a Welsh gentleman," he added. H. L. Mencken, "The Sahara of Bozart," in *American Essays*, ed. Charles B. Shaw (New York: Pelican Mentor Books, 1948), 118.

4. Gail Godwin, "The Southern Belle," *Ms.*, July 1975, 49.

5. Florence King, *Confessions of a Failed Southern Lady* (New York: St. Martin's/Marek, 1985), 1.

6. Tom Wolfe, *The Kandy-Kolored Tangerine-Flake Streamline Baby* (New York: Pocket Books, 1966), 108.

7. Immanuel Wallerstein, "Some Reflections on History, the Social Sciences, and Politics," in *The Capitalist World-Economy* (Cambridge: Cambridge University Press, 1979), x–xi.

8. Weber's remarks on ideal types are scattered throughout his works. For a good summary, see Julien Freund, *The Sociology of Max Weber* (New York: Vintage Books, 1969), 59–70.

9. The basic idea of labeling theory was adumbrated by Howard Becker, in *Outsiders: Studies in the Sociology of Deviance* (Glencoe, Ill.: Free Press, 1963), especially 19–39; it can be found more fully developed in Thomas J. Scheff, *Being Mentally Ill: A Sociological Theory* (Chicago: Aldine, 1966), 55–101.

10. Stanley Elkins, *Slavery: A Problem in American Institutional and Intellectual Life*, 3d ed. (Chicago: University of Chicago Press, 1976), 81–139, especially 81–89 and 115–33; quotations from 82, 123, 125, 131.

11. W. J. Cash, *The Mind of the South* (New York: Alfred A. Knopf, 1941), 68.

12. Quoted in Marshall Frady, *Wallace* (New York: New American Library, 1975), 229. (A good old boy would have known that Wallace was talking about *Bruton* snuff.) Wallace also told Frady about a woman named Kathryn Renfroe, "a beautiful girl," member of the Socialist League in Denver, who "decided she'd make a study of us hillbillies. We let her study on us a little bit."

13. Tindall, *The Ethnic Southerners*, 41.

14. George Core has written about these factors as they affect the writing of fiction, in "The Literary Marketplace and the Southern Writer Today," *Southern Review* 21 (April 1985): 306–7. When a writer succumbs to them, Core argues, he "prostitutes his art and becomes a sociologist or a propagandist or both" (306). I am arguing instead that he becomes *data* for a sociologist, but that may sound even more unpleasant.

15. Introduction to *The South and Film*, ed. Warren French (Jackson: University Press of Mississippi, 1981), 6. Floyd Watkins makes a case for the stereotyped and propagandistic fiction of the civil rights era—e.g., the novels of Jesse Hill Ford—as *the* classic "Southern," with issues "just about as superficial and clear-cut as when the ugly villain tries to foreclose the mortgage on the beautiful and helpless damsel who has inherited her father's ranch" in the classic Western (*The Death of Art* [1970], quoted in Core, "The Literary Marketplace"). But I believe there are too many competing formulas. Several of the chapters in French's book are very much to the point here, although most have a cineastic emphasis on individual directors or particular movies. See especially Wade Austin's "The Real Beverly Hillbillies"; " 'Burn, Mandingo, Burn': The Plantation South in Film, 1958–1978," by Edward D. C. Campbell, Jr.; Victoria O'Donnell's "The Southern Woman as Time-Binder in Film"; and Lenora Clodfelter Stephens's, "Black Women in Film." Two excellent books on the subject are Jack Temple Kirby, *Media-Made Dixie: The South in the American Imagination* (Baton Rouge: Louisiana State University Press, 1978), and Edward D. C. Campbell, Jr., *The Celluloid South: The Old South in American Film, 1903–1978* (Knoxville: University of Tennessee Press, 1981). See also Peter A. Soderbergh, "Hollywood and the South, 1930–1960," *Mississippi Quarterly* 19 (Winter 1965–1966): 1–19, and Fred Chappell, "The Image of the South in Film," *Southern Humanities Review* 12 (Fall 1978): 303–11.

16. Compared to all the attention to the cinematic South, there has been relatively

little examination of television's treatment of the region. Kirby discusses it in *Media-Made Dixie*, and revises his view somewhat in "The Southern 'Catch 22,'" *Southern Partisan*, Fall 1981, 10–12. Marsha G. McGee presents an excellent summary and discussion in "Prime-Time Dixie: Television's View of a 'Simple' South," *Journal of American Culture* 6 (Fall 1983): 100–109, and Eric Peter Verschuure complains about one common image in "Stumble, Bumble, Mumble: TV's Image of the South," *Journal of Popular Culture* 16 (Winter 1982): 92–96, as does Roy Blount, Jr., in "C'mon, They're Not All Dumber than Two-Dollar Dogs," *TV Guide*, 2 February 1980, 4–8. Many have found television hillbillies to be particularly offensive. See below, page 96, notes 40–43.

17. The *Southern Partisan* (Fall 1984, 1) was quoting Richard Weaver's definition of conservativism.

18. The classic critique remains Daniel J. Boorstin, *The Image; or, What Happened to the American Dream* (New York: Atheneum, 1962). See especially Boorstin's chapter, "From Hero to Celebrity: The Human Pseudo-Event," 45–76.

19. Bill AuCoin, *Redneck* (Matteson, Ill.: Greatlakes Living Press, 1977).

20. Veblen's view and others are summarized in Quentin Bell's engaging treatise *On Human Finery*, rev. ed. (New York: Schocken Books, 1976), chapter four ("Theories of Fashion"), 90–106.

21. Aaron Latham, "The Ballad of the Urban Cowboy: America's Search for True Grit," *Esquire*, 12 September 1978, 21–30.

22. Athan Manuel, J. S. Reed, and Charles R. Wilson, "*Playboy*'s Southern Exposure," in *Perspectives on the American South: An Annual Review of Politics, Culture, and Society*, vol. 4, ed. James Cobb and Charles R. Wilson (New York: Gordon & Breach, Science Publishers, in press).

23. Ibid.

24. Walker Percy, *Lancelot* (New York: Avon Books, 1977), 128.

25. Robert Sherrill, "The Pork Chop Conspiracy," *New York Times Magazine*, 10 October 1976, 111.

26. Robert K. Merton, "Insiders and Outsiders: A Chapter in the Sociology of Knowledge," *American Journal of Sociology* 78 (July 1972): 9–47. Merton makes the point, worth emphasizing, that outsiders' perceptions are not necessarily inferior, but they are usually different.

27. On the tradition of Staggerlee, "Nobody's fool, nobody's man, tougher than the devil and out of God's reach," see Marcus, *Mystery Train*, 75–111, 233–38 (quote from 78).

28. Irving Lewis Allen, *The Language of Ethnic Conflict: Social Organization and Lexical Culture* (New York: Columbia University Press, 1983), 68.
29. Robert K. Merton, *Social Theory and Social Structure*, rev. ed. (Glencoe, Ill.: Free Press, 1957), 421–36.
30. The findings are Gail Wood's, reported in John Shelton Reed, "Getting to Know You: The 'Contact Hypothesis' Applied to the Sectional Beliefs and Attitudes of White Southerners," *Social Forces* 59 (September 1980): 123–35.
31. Robert M. Pierce, "Jimmy Carter and the New South: The View from New York," in *Perspectives on the American South: An Annual Review of Politics, Culture, and Society*, vol. 2, ed. Merle Black and J. S. Reed (New York: Gordon & Breach, Science Publishers, 1984).
32. Quoted in Tindall, *The Ethnic Southerners*, 30. See also 24–25 for a couple of stories that illustrate the point.
33. Edwin M. Yoder, Jr. *The Night of the Old South Ball, and Other Essays and Fables* (Oxford, Miss.: Yoknapatawpha Press, 1984), 198–99. A discussion of the vital role of "working mythologists" in maintaining national awareness of the South and even regional *self*-consciousness is on p. 72.
34. For a book-length review, see Fred Hobson, *Tell About the South: The Southern Rage to Explain* (Baton Rouge: Louisiana State University Press, 1983). Stephen A. Smith's fine study, *Myth, Media, and the Southern Mind* (Fayetteville: University of Arkansas Press, 1985) appeared too late for this essay to profit from it, but it is very much to my point here, and elsewhere.
35. McGee, "Prime-Time Dixie," 100.
36. Percy, *Lancelot*, 26–27.
37. Quoted in Frady, *Wallace*, 229–30.

Chapter Two

1. Kirby, "The Southern 'Catch 22,'" 11.
2. Or so we can conclude from the fascinating work of Charles Osgood and his colleagues (Charles E. Osgood, George J. Suci, and Percy H. Tannenbaum, *The Measurement of Meaning* [Urbana: University of Illinois Press, 1957]). A third dimension, roughly fast-slow, does not seem to distinguish among Southern regional types, each of which is, in its own way, slow. In fact, slowness appears to be *the* characteristic "Southern" trait: see John Shelton Reed, "Life and Leisure in the New South," *North Carolina Historical Review* 60 (April 1983): 172–82.

3. These lines, reported in Thomas Talley's *Negro Folk Rhymes* (1922), are quoted in Archie Green, "Hillbilly Music: Source and Symbol," *Journal of American Folklore* 78 (July–September 1965): 204.

4. Nearly all social types have at least an implicit sex and ethnicity. Some countercultural types (e.g., bohemian, beatnik, hippie) may be equal-opportunity categories with regard to sex, and so may some *very* recent (that is, post-feminist) types: e.g., preppie, yuppie, or punk (in its latest sense). But these are exceptions to what seems to be a rule. Moreover, I cannot think offhand of any social-type labels that could apply to either race, but apply to blacks by assumption, or any that apply to females by default but could also apply to males. In other words, the default *person* appears to be a white male, here as elsewhere.

5. Although this may be changing, and we have almost no evidence on the subject anyway. See Merle Black and John Shelton Reed, "Blacks and Southerners: A Research Note," *Journal of Politics* 44 (February 1982): 165–71.

6. And also in contrast to the same students' readiness to generalize about "typical" traits of white Southerners and Northerners. (John Shelton Reed, *The Enduring South: Subcultural Persistence in Mass Society* [Lexington, Mass.: D. C. Heath, 1972], 26–28.)

7. Allen, *The Language of Ethnic Conflict*, 68.

8. Mary R. Jackman and Robert W. Jackman, *Class Awareness in the United States* (Berkeley: University of California Press, 1983), report that Americans generally discern five social classes: upper, upper-middle, middle, working, and lower. Many community studies in the small-town and rural South, however, have found only three. For example, the mountain folk studied by Burton Kaplan in *Blue Ridge: An Appalachian Community in Transition* (Morgantown: Appalachian Center, West Virginia University, 1971) sorted each other into "betters," "get-bys," and "sorries." Similarly, the white population of "Kent," a south Carolina mill town, was divided into "bluebloods," "plain people," and "trashy people" (Ralph C. Patrick, Jr., "A Cultural Approach to Stratification" [Ph.D. diss., Harvard University, 1953]). From the top or outside, though, even the distinction between plain and trashy—i.e., between working and lower classes—is blurred (or, rather, it becomes a moral rather than an economic judgment). See Cash, *The Mind of the South*, 282–83.

9. This makes social-type images different from, say, occupational stereotypes. Even people who dislike the idea of male nurses or female stockbrokers do not deny that the people they are dealing with *are* nurses and stockbrokers. But

no anti-discrimination laws apply to social types. If the *vox populi* says you have to be male to be a geezer or a slob, or white to be a wimp, there is no recourse.

10. For white male types, the two cognitive dimensions, good—bad and strong—weak, correspond closely to two of Max Weber's three dimensions of class (prestige and power), while what I am calling "social class" corresponds roughly to the third (wealth). See Max Weber, "Class, Status, Party," in *From Max Weber: Essays in Sociology,* ed. H. H. Gerth and C. Wright Mills (New York: Oxford University Press, 1958), 180–95. (I thank Charles Warren for pointing this out to me.) Sex and race, of course, are two other fundamental bases for social stratification. This means that the matrix of Southern regional types is a very *sociological* one, compared to Klapp's listing of American types which seem much more often to be psychological types. This may reflect the Southern types' origins in a relatively settled, agrarian culture, where race, sex, and social position were of more determinative importance than they have since become.

11. On this accommodation, see D. K. Wilgus, "Country-Western Music and the Urban Hillbilly," *Journal of American Folklore* 83 (April–June 1970); 175–79.

12. Daniel R. Hundley, *Social Relations in Our Southern States* (1860; reprint ed., Baton Rouge: Louisiana State University Press, 1979, with a useful introduction by William J. Cooper, Jr.). Hundley has received surprisingly little attention from historians. (Hobson, *Tell About the South,* 63–64, offers a review—and Hobson's own discussion (63–81) is an exception.) He has received even less attention from sociologists, who should probably count him as some sort of an uncle, if not a forefather. Tommy W. Rogers is the only sociologist, to my knowledge, who has written about Hundley, and he did not write in journals many sociologists are likely to read: "D. R. Hundley: A Multi-Class Thesis of Social Stratification in the Antebellum South," *Mississippi Quarterly* 23 (Spring 1970): 135–54, and "Daniel Hundley's Contribution to Folklore," *Alabama Historical Quarterly* 30 (Fall–Winter 1968): 203–18. See also Blanche H. C. Weaver, "D. R. Hundley: Subjective Sociologist," *Georgia Review* 10 (Summer 1956): 222–34. A recent enterprise with much the same goal as Hundley's, and one remarkably similar in the resulting portrait, is F. N. Boney, *Southerners All* (Macon: Mercer University Press, 1984).

13. A seventh chapter is devoted to the Southern middle classes (see below, 63–77), and an eighth to Southern blacks.

14. The gentleman's characteristics have not changed appreciably since Hundley's

time. For good discussions of the historical type, see the chapter, "Gentility," in Bertram Wyatt-Brown, *Southern Honor: Ethics and Behavior in the Old South* (New York: Oxford University Press, 1982): 88–114; and F. N. Boney, "The Southern Aristocrat," *Midwest Quarterly* 15 (Spring 1974): 215–30.

15. Francis Pendleton Gaines, *The Southern Plantation: A Study in the Development and the Accuracy of a Tradition* (New York: Columbia University Press, 1925), especially 1–142 on the development of the myth in literature, on the stage, and in popular song.

16. "Yet [Virginians do] not lack the grace to acknowledge worth or merit in another, wherever the native place of that other: for it is a common thing to hear them say of a neighbor: 'He is a clever fellow, *though* he *did* come from New Jersey, or even Connecticut.'" Joseph G. Baldwin, *The Flush Times of Alabama and Mississippi* (1853; reprint ed., Gloucester, Mass.: Peter Smith, 1974), 54.

17. So Louis D. Rubin, Jr., has speculated, at least, in *The Wary Fugitives: Four Poets and the South* (Baton Rouge: Louisiana State University Press, 1978), 297–301.

18. Connelly, *The Marble Man*.

19. Stephen A. Smith, "The Old South Myth as a Contemporary Southern Commodity," *The Journal of Popular Culture* 16 (Winter 1982): 22–29; quotation from 24.

20. Charles R. Wilson, *Baptized in Blood: The Religion of the Lost Cause, 1865–1920* (Athens: University of Georgia Press, 1980).

21. He received about one vote in five, far outdistancing George Wallace and Billy Graham, who tied for second place. John Shelton Reed, *Southerners: The Social Psychology of Sectionalism* (Chapel Hill: University of North Carolina Press, 1983), 85.

22. Helper's views, as those of an anti-slavery North Carolinian, reflected not regional but class antagonism. "The lords of the lash are not only absolute masters of the blacks, who are bought and sold, and driven about like so many cattle, but they are also the oracles and arbiters of all non-slaveholding whites, whose freedom is purely nominal." (*The Impending Crisis of the South: How to Meet It*, quoted in Edmund Wilson, *Patriotic Gore: Studies in the Literature of the American Civil War* [New York: Oxford University Press, 1966], 371.)

23. Tindall, *The Ethnic Southerners*, 27–29.

24. The analogy is Fred Hawley's, from "The Black Legend in Southern Studies" (Paper presented to the annual meeting of the Mid-South Sociological Associa-

tion, Jackson, Mississippi, 1982). And, of course, antebellum Southerners constructed their own unflattering image of the North, but that does not concern us here.

25. See, for instance, Howard R. Floan, *The South in Northern Eyes, 1831 to 1861* (New York: McGraw-Hill, 1958), or James B. Colvert, "Views of Southern Character in Some Northern Novels," *Mississippi Quarterly* 18 (Spring 1965): 59–68. Phillips is quoted in Floan, p. 14.

26. According to Hundley, the "most utterly detestable" of the type, "preeminent in villainy and a greedy love of filthy lucre, [is] the hard-hearted Negro Trader, . . . as unconscionable a dog of a Southern Shylock as ever . . . used New England cowskins to lacerate the back of a slave" (*Social Relations*, 139–40).

27. Howard W. Odum, *The Way of the South: Toward the Regional Balance of America* (New York: Macmillan, 1947), 197–207.

28. For examinations of a number of civil-rights era Southern politicians in this light, emphasizing their "devastating incompetence and cheap trickery," see Robert Sherrill, *Gothic Politics in the Deep South: Stars of the New Confederacy* (New York: Ballantine Books, 1969); quotation from page 3. Sherrill recognizes the mythic dimensions of his subject; of Leander Perez, he writes: "There is something about [him], perhaps best described as the gargoyles of his mind, that is not unkin to the misshapen, magical, evil creatures of medieval mythology. One is constantly expecting him to resume the shape of a toad" (8).

29. George B. Tindall, "Sunbelt Snow Job," *Houston Review* 1 (Spring 1979): 3–13.

30. The *New Yorker* articles became a book: Kirkpatrick Sale, *Power Shift: The Rise of the Southern Rim and Its Challenge to the Eastern Establishment* (New York: Vintage Books, 1976).

31. "'Terrible Ted': Turner's Bid for CBS Viewed as Outlandish, Fits In With His Image," *Wall Street Journal*, 19 April 1985, 1, 6.

32. This genealogy is the one Hundley provided for the Southern middle classes, but that is where he believed that most Southern Yankees originated (*Social Relations*, 131).

33. Wyatt-Brown, *Southern Honor*. See, e.g., 33–35, 148–74.

34. Ibid., 99–105. We shall have to wait for Wyatt-Brown's next two books for a fuller treatment.

35. Walker Percy, *Lancelot*, 122, 231.

36. Florence King, *Southern Ladies and Gentlemen* (New York: Bantam Books, 1976), 156–71, quotation from 157.
37. Ibid., 169.

Chapter Three

1. Again, page numbers in the text refer to Hundley, *Social Relations*.
2. Hundley volunteered that these "evils . . . in most cases have their origin in a disordered stomach."
3. Plantation overseers were largely drawn from this class, according to Hundley, who compared that much-abused occupation favorably to Northern policemen (*Social Relations*, 203–7).
4. Cash, *The Mind of the South*, 50.
5. Wolfe's article is reprinted in his collection, *The Kandy-Kolored Tangerine-Flake Streamline Baby*. The description of the good old boy is on page 108.
6. Florence King, "The Good Ole Boy," *Harper's*, May 1974, 78. Why King chose to spell "old" phonetically is not clear to me.
7. "I can count on my fingers without seriously affecting my typing speed the Southern men I have known who are not Good Ole Boys." (ibid., 79, 82.) Elsewhere, King has even suggested that Richard Nixon was one (*Southern Ladies and Gentlemen*, 103). I suspect she got carried away: perhaps she meant to say that he sometimes *tried* to be one.
8. (His brother, yes.) Johnny Greene, "The Dixie Smile," *Harper's*, September 1976, 14, 19. We have it on the authority of the *Washington Star* that Billy Carter was "a Good Old Boy as Southern as sawmill gravy and fried white meat." (Michael Satchell, "Jimmy's Brother Billy: 'I'm a Real Southern Boy,'" reprinted in the *Raleigh News and Observer*, 15 November 1976, 1.) On Jimmy, see even the title of William Lee Miller, *Yankee from Georgia: The Emergence of Jimmy Carter* (New York: Time Books, 1978). *Time* magazine, to its credit, understood the difference between Billy and Jimmy, although it could not resist overdoing it: e.g., "for state occasions," the good old boy wears "a leisure suit with a colored shirt" ("Those Good Ole Boys," *Time*, 27 September 1976, 47).
9. Greene, "The Dixie Smile," 19.
10. Walker Percy, "Questions They Never Asked Me," *Esquire*, December 1977, 170.
11. Pat Nunnally, "The South Created: Image Making in the National Press" (Un-

published paper, Vanderbilt University, 1980). *Why* the early 1970s should have been an era of sectional good-feeling is another question, and an interesting one. See J. R. Vanover, "The Useful South," *Southern Partisan*, April 1980, 38, for some speculation.

12. Ingram Parmley, "Stalking the Good Old Boy," in *Perspectives on the American South*, vol. 1, ed. Merle Black and J. S. Reed (New York: Gordon & Breach, Science Publishers, 1981). Parmley's article is a model for the sort of research that could be done on each of these regional social types, or any other social type for that matter.

13. Roy Blount, Jr., *Crackers: This Whole Many-Angled Thing of Jimmy, More Carters, Ominous Little Animals, Sad-Singing Women, My Daddy and Me* (New York: Alfred A. Knopf, 1980), 71, 70.

14. Thompson, "Decency," 434–46.

15. Blount, *Crackers*, 76. Actually, the one Jimmy Carter story I know that reveals any good-old-boyish qualities has to do with a promise he made while running for governor that he would build a nuclear reactor at Georgia Tech. A couple of years after his election there was no sign of a reactor, and he was reminded of his promise. "I'm just a country boy," he told the Georgia Tech scientists, "and you city boys never did understand the way we talk." (Greene, "The Dixie Smile," 19.)

16. Last names would have been out of place in that sentence, but let me identify these couples here: Burt Reynolds and Jerry Reed, good old stars of a number of type-propagating movies; Bo and Luke Duke, good old brothers on the "Dukes of Hazzard" television program; Moe Bandy and Joe Stampley, good old country-music singers who recorded (among many other songs) "Just Good Ol' Boys"; Hamilton Jordan and Jody Powell, good old presidential assistants in the Carter White House and cover boys for *Rolling Stone* magazine.

17. Blount, *Crackers*, 71.

18. Larry L. King, "We Ain't Trash No More," *Esquire*, November 1976, 156.

19. Quoted in Jeremy Rifkin and Ted Howard, *Redneck Power: The Wit and Wisdom of Billy Carter* (New York: Bantam Books, 1977). I thank Ingram Parmley for this precious citation.

20. Common usage does not always distinguish between the positive "good old boy" and the negative "redneck." Using the two labels more or less interchangeably sometimes reflects simple ignorance. But other times the confusion is deliberate, by those who believe that men commonly styled good old boys are not *that* good, or that those commonly labeled rednecks are not *that* bad. Paul Hemphill, for example, points to good old boys' "dark side" of racism

and violence (quoted in Parmley, "Stalking the Good Old Boy," 338), and Florence King and Johnny Greene clearly dislike many men they regard as good old boys. On the other hand, Will D. Campbell has written a moving and empathetic account of those called rednecks (in "The World of the Redneck," *Katallagete* 5 [Spring 1974]: 34–40), as have Julian B. Roebuck and his colleagues (Roebuck and Ronald L. Neff, "The Multiple Reality of the 'Redneck': Toward a Grounded Theory of the Southern Class Structure," *Studies in Symbolic Interaction* 3 [1980]: 233–62; Roebuck and Mark Hickson III, *The Southern Redneck: A Phenomenological Case Study* [New York: Praeger Publishers, 1982]). These writers are discussing actual people, who are of course a mixture of the good and bad: social types are purer. As a type, the good old boy embodies Southern working-class virtue: the label is an in-group term of approval. The redneck, as a type, *is* the good old boy's "dark side." No one could deny that the phrase "good old boy" was originally meant to be complimentary, nor would anyone deny that "redneck" has negative connotations.

21. F. N. Boney, "The Redneck," *Georgia Review* 25 (Fall 1971): 333. Boney is particularly perceptive about the transmutation of the redneck's villainous traits into evidence of victimization when they are displayed by other down-and-out groups (335–36). This "moral alchemy" is a variation on the process Robert K. Merton was discussing when he coined that phrase, in *Social Theory and Social Structure*, 426–30.

22. To be precise, this is the *poor* Southern Bully. Hundley described a (less numerous) rich variety as well, which he saw as typically the wastrel son of the Southern Yankee, not socially ambitious enough to be a Cotton Snob. He proposed that these men be encouraged to filibuster and conquer Central America, and then to settle it, raising the tone both of the South and of Central America (*Social Relations*, 248–49).

23. "Schuylers, Huntingtons, and other *gentlemen* of the like kidney, presidents of banks, coal companies, railroad corporations, et cetera, et cetera; who are every day growing rich on the hard earnings of the poor, pilfering from the day laborers, and absolutely stealing the little savings intrusted to them by toiling servant-girls [etc.]." As a Harvard-trained lawyer, Hundley may have known what he was talking about.

24. Hundley digressed into entertaining but rather beside-the-point descriptions of white tavern-keepers and horse-traders, and of black barmaids. He apparently disapproved of all about equally (*Social Relations*, 226–36). In his opinion, taverns and groggeries encouraged race-mixing and dissipation.

25. Raymond S. Rodgers, "Images of Rednecks in Country Music: The Lyrical Per-

sona of a Southern Superman," *Journal of Regional Cultures* 1 (Fall–Winter 1981): 75. Q: Why do rednecks fight in parking lots? A: Somebody's got to do it. (Paraphrased from Don Addis, "Real Men Don't Eat Kwitchy," *The Floridian* [supplement to *St. Petersburg Times*], 11 July 1982, 5.)

26. Florence King, "Red Necks, White Socks, and Blue Ribbon Fear," *Harper's*, July 1974, 31; Richard Goldstein, "My Country Music Problem—and Yours," *Mademoiselle*, June 1973, 115. Goldstein's article is not as stupid as these out-of-context quotations make it sound. James C. Cobb has written about this revaluation, with particular reference to country music, in "From Muskogee to Luckenbach: Country Music and the 'Southernization' of America," *Journal of Popular Culture* 16 (Winter 1982): 81–91, from which the Goldstein and King citations have been taken.

27. Joe Bob Briggs's syndicated column itself conveys an image of Southern (or at least Texas) manhood. This quotation is taken from a column headlined "Joe Bob issues a Communist Alert for Massillon," in the *Cleveland Plain Dealer*, 29 March 1985, 12.

28. "[T]he Poor Whites of the South constitute a separate class to themselves," Hundley wrote. But he went on to add that "the Southern Yeomen are as distinct from them as the Southern Gentleman is from the Cotton Snob" (*Social Relations*, 193).

29. Merrill Maguire Skaggs, in *The Folk of Southern Fiction* (Athens: University of Georgia Press, 1972), 142–43, discusses the distinction in literature between poor whites and "the plain man." This distinction among non-genteel whites is still widespread, at least among non-genteel whites. See above, page 88, note 8.

30. On the history of the word "hillbilly," see Archie Green, "Hillbilly Music," 204.

31. Lewis Killian, *White Southerners* (New York: Random House, 1970), 100. On some of the myths specifically attached to the Southern mountains, see Henry D. Shapiro, *Appalachia on Our Mind: The Southern Mountains and Mountaineers in the American Consciousness, 1870–1920* (Chapel Hill: University of North Carolina Press, 1978).

32. For a good review, see David Bertelson, *The Lazy South* (New York: Oxford University Press, 1967).

33. He added that "there is a great deal more in *blood* than people in the United States are generally inclined to believe."

34. Hundley referred to snuff-dipping as a "filthy and disgusting vice," and observed that it had spread to women of the yeoman and even the middle classes in some parts of the South, "particularly in North-Carolina."

35. He insisted that Southern Congressmen as a rule had "more of good breeding, of gentlemanly bearing, of chivalric tone and statesmanlike deportment" than their Northern colleagues, but allowed that even in 1860 a few were "tippling, gambling, and debauched libertines" (*Social Relations*, 269). He blamed these exceptions on the votes of Poor White Trash.

36. The classic work on this social type's treatment in literature is Shields McIlwaine's 1939 book, *The Southern Poor-White from Lubberland to Tobacco Road* (reprint ed., New York: Cooper Square Publishers, 1970). For a more recent treatment, see Sylvia Jenkins Cook, *From Tobacco Road to Route 66: The Southern Poor White in Fiction* (Chapel Hill: University of North Carolina Press, 1976).

37. Green, "Hillbilly Music," offers an interesting account. See also Wilgus, "Country-Western Music," 175–79.

38. McGee, "Prime Time Dixie," 101, 103.

39. WRAL-TV sources, quoted in *The Spectator* [Raleigh, N.C.], 13 June 1985, S3.

40. John Egerton and Frye Gaillard, "The Mountaineer Minority," *Race Relations Reporter*, March 1974, 8.

41. David E. Whisnant, "Ethnicity and the Recovery of Regional Identity in Appalachia: Thoughts upon Entering the Zone of Occult Instability," *Soundings: An Interdisciplinary Journal* 56 (Spring 1973): 129. Whisnant professed to find it strange that "Networks which have long since discontinued 'Amos 'n' Andy' and other racist programs and which have shown some signs recently of redressing their sexist images of women, continue to run such shows."

42. James Branscome, "Annihilating the Hillbilly: The Appalachians' Struggle with America's Institutions," *Katallagete* 3 (Winter 1971): 25. Like Whisnant, like Egerton and Gaillard, and presumably like most Southerners, Branscome saw the objectionable comic strips and television programs as specifically *Appalachian* in provenance. It is ironic that non-Southerners, for the most part, apparently do not distinguish between upland and lowland South. See above, pp. 42–43.

43. Horace Newcomb seems to be less unhinged by the subject than most other commentators. See his "Appalachia on Television: Region as Symbol in American Popular Culture," *Appalachian Journal* 7 (Autumn–Winter 1979–80): 155–64. See also McGee, "Prime Time Dixie."

44. Blount, "Two-Dollar Dogs," 5–6.

45. Ibid., 8.

46. Erskine Caldwell and Margaret Bourke-White, *You Have Seen Their Faces* (New York: Modern Age Books, 1937).

47. James Agee and Walker Evans, *Let Us Now Praise Famous Men* (Boston: Houghton Mifflin, 1941).

48. For a more reverent view, see Hart Wegner, "A Chronicle of Soil, Seasons and Weather: Jean Renoir's *The Southerner,*" in *The South and Film,* ed. French.

49. Some scholars have been exceptions, but they have had an up-hill struggle. For the classic revision of the historical record, see Frank Lawrence Owsley, *Plain Folk of the Old South* (Baton Rouge: Louisiana State University Press, 1949). Treatments of the contemporary situation include Wayne Flynt, *Dixie's Forgotten People: The South's Poor Whites* (Bloomington: Indiana University Press, 1979) and Boney, *Southerners All,* 31–67.

50. John Shelton Reed, *One South: An Ethnic Approach to Regional Culture* (Baton Rouge: Louisiana State University Press, 1982), 171–83.

51. Barbara B. Sims, " 'She's Got to be a Saint, Lord Knows I Ain't': Feminine Masochism in American Country Music," *Journal of Country Music* 5 (Spring 1974): 24. (Sims appears to be quoting Wilgus, from "Country-Western Music," but I cannot locate the phrase in Wilgus. Nevertheless, see 176–78 for a discussion of this genre.) Katie Letcher Lyle reported that 36 of the top 100 country songs in early 1977 were about cheating ("Southern Country Music: A Brief Eulogy," in *The American South: Portrait of a Culture,* ed. Louis D. Rubin, Jr. [Baton Rouge: Louisiana State University Press, 1980], 143). See also Jimmie N. Rogers, *The Country Music Message: All About Lovin' and Livin'* (Englewood Cliffs, N.J.: Prentice-Hall, 1983), 89–114; C. R. Chandler and H. Paul Chalfant, "The Sexual Double Standard in Country Music Song Lyrics," *Free Inquiry in Creative Sociology* 13 (November 1985), 155–59; and C. R. Chandler, H. Paul Chalfant, and Craig P. Chalfant, "Cheaters Sometimes Win: Sexual Infidelity in Country Music," in *Forbidden Fruits: Taboos and Tabooism in Culture,* ed. Ray B. Browne (Bowling Green, Ohio: Bowling Green University Popular Press, 1984).

Chapter Four

1. King, *Southern Ladies and Gentlemen,* 103–15.

2. All of the regional types seem to be adult types, at least in default: they evoke grown-up images. I do not believe we have a typology for Southern children apart from them. White Southern children are sorted as incipient grown-ups. Girls are little ladies: boys are little gentlemen, or little rednecks. There is no white Southern equivalent even for the pickaninny.

3. Anne Firor Scott, *The Southern Lady: From Pedestal to Politics, 1830–1930* (Chicago: University of Chicago Press, 1970), 4.

4. Francis Pendleton Gaines, quoted in Tindall, *The Ethnic Southerners*, 26.

5. For some of the other possibilities, see Tristram Potter Coffin, *The Female Hero in Folklore and Legend* (New York: Seabury Press, 1975).

6. Margaret Ripley Wolfe, "The Southern Lady: Long Suffering Counterpart of the Good Ole Boy," *Journal of Popular Culture* 11 (Summer 1977): 25, 26.

7. Godwin, "The Southern Belle," 85.

8. This I conclude from Scott, *The Southern Lady*. In any case, submissiveness may be going out of fashion without the lady's thereby ceasing to exist. Gayle J. Rogers argues for the lady's increasing "vigor and independence" (indeed, that she is becoming a "self-realizing performer") in "The Changing Image of the Southern Woman: A Performer on a Pedestal," *Journal of Popular Culture* 16 (Winter 1982): 66.

9. King, *Southern Ladies and Gentlemen*, 198–224.

10. Chappell, "The South in Film," 310. Chappell points out that "almost any film with a Scarlett-like character will offer its obverse" (311). A marvelous collection of critical and scholarly response to Margaret Mitchell's mythogenic creation can be found in Darden A. Pyron, *Recasting: "Gone with the Wind" in American Culture* (Gainesville: University Presses of Florida, 1983).

11. Clance quoted in Sharon McKern, *Redneck Mothers, Good Ol' Girls and Other Southern Belles: A Celebration of the Women of Dixie* (New York: Viking Press, 1979), 68–69; ibid., 8–9. The operative word in McKern's title is "celebration": her book, like its stereotypical subject, is relentlessly upbeat and sometimes cloyingly cute, but it is fundamentally serious in purpose (as King's *Southern Ladies and Gentlemen* is not) and contains much valuable material.

12. Chappell, "The South in Film," 309. See his discussion of portrayals of the South as "the Hell of Sexual Confusion."

13. Marshall Frady, "Skirmishes with the Ladies of the Magnolias," *Playboy*, September 1972, 216.

14. See above, pp. 27–28; Campbell, *The Celluloid South*, 171–79, and " 'Burn, Mandingo, Burn': The Plantation South in Film, 1958–1978," in *The South and Film*, ed. French, 107–16.

15. To borrow some choice words from Kirby, "The Southern 'Catch 22,' " 12.

16. Helen Brown Norden, *The Hussy's Handbook*, rev. ed. (New York: Arden, 1944), 50, 51.

17. The context makes it clear that he is speaking of ladies, and especially of young ones. Frady, "Skirmishes," 216.
18. Quoted in McGee, "Prime Time Dixie," 104.
19. Manuel, Reed, and Wilson, "*Playboy*'s Southern Exposure."
20. D. Harland Hagler, "The Ideal Woman in the Antebellum South: Lady or Farmwife?" *Journal of Southern History* 46 (August 1980): 405–18.
21. Ruth A. Banes, "Southern Women in Country Songs," *Journal of Regional Cultures* 1 (Fall–Winter 1982): 57–70; "Continuity and Change in the Myth of the Southern Woman: Country Women and Rhinestone Cowgirls" (Paper presented at conference on Southern women, Georgia State University, 6 March 1981); "Mythology in Music: The Ballad of Loretta Lynn," *Canadian Review of American Studies* (in press). Recent country music offers many more songs from women's point of view; in the older version, women scarcely existed except in relation to men. See Robert K. Oerman, "Mother, Sister, Sweetheart, Pal: Women in Old-Time Country Music," *Southern Quarterly* 12 (Spring 1984): 125–34.
22. Michael Hicks, *The South Made Simple* (Austin: Texas Monthly Press, 1982). Hicks's book is in the humorous-guidebook genre, but differs from many others in that it actually *is* funny, in spots. Compare it, for instance, to Lewis Green, *How Tuh Live in the Kooky South Without Eatin' Grits: A Fun Guide Book fer Yankees* (Highlands, N.C.: The Merry Mountaineers, 1978). Only two things are amusing about Green's book: (1) some sections cribbed without attribution from King's *Southern Ladies and Gentlemen*, and (2) the thought of Northern tourists paying $1.75 for it.
23. Mary Bufwack, "The Feminist Sensibility in Post-War Country Music," *Southern Quarterly* 12 (Spring 1984): 135–44.
24. Sims, "'She's Got to Be a Saint,'" 24–30. On conflicting images of women in country music, see Brenda J. Vander Mey, "Southern Women and Country Music: Myths, Messages, and Contradictory Imagery" (Unpublished paper, Department of Sociology, Clemson University, n.d.); also Vander Mey and Ellen S. Bryant, "Southern Sex Roles: Country Music as the Vehicle for Investigation," (Paper presented at meeting of the Southern Sociological Society, Atlanta, April 1983).
25. "Cheatin' Men & Sufferin' Women," *Woman's Day*, 4 November 1980, 22.
26. Which gives me a long-sought excuse to cite George William Koon, "Tammy Wynette and the Objective Correlative," *Studies in Popular Culture* 6 (1983): 47–52.

27. Rogers, *The Country Music Message*, is far and away the most extensive treatment of this and other themes in country music.

28. Ibid. Rogers discusses the various permutations. See also above, page 47, and the works cited there.

29. Bill Crider, "Sons of *Tobacco Road:* 'Backwoods' Novels," *Journal of Popular Culture* 16 (Winter 1982): 47–59. The photographs of book-jackets accompanying Crider's article make the point even more obviously than the titles. Skaggs, in *The Folk of Southern Fiction*, 151–53, argues that the mountain girls of local color fiction, though seldom explicitly promiscuous, were often implicitly so.

30. All of these characteristics, of course, are also aspects of white Southerners' (and other white Americans') traditional derogatory stereotype of blacks, and the same analysis can be applied. Id stereotypes are distinguished from the "superego" stereotypes, involving cunning and treachery, often affixed to commercial or merchant populations. (The derogatory Southern stereotype of Yankees is in many respects a superego stereotype.) Which sort of unacceptable impulses gets projected depends on the relative structural positions of the two groups, but the psychological functions of the projection are the same in either case. See Thomas F. Pettigrew, "Complexity and Change in American Racial Patterns: A Social Psychological View," in *The Negro American*, ed. Talcott Parsons and Kenneth B. Clark (Boston: Beacon Press, 1967), 348–49.

Chapter Five

1. Hundley, *Social Relations*, 77–128. The quotations following are from 78–80.

2. He described a number of different *occupational* social types, but that is not the same thing.

3. Much of this discussion is adapted from "Grits and Gravy: The South's New Middle Class," in Reed, *One South*.

4. Ibid. See also Reed, *Southerners*.

5. Reed, *The Enduring South*, and "The *Prevailing* South?" *National Humanities Center Newsletter* 5, no. 4 (Summer 1984): 1–7.

6. Woodward, "Southern Styles," 1. In this address to a Southern audience (not published elsewhere, so far as I know), Woodward had some other pointed observations on this subject.

7. This reference and those following are to Kirby, "The Southern 'Catch 22,' " 11.

8. Vanover, "The Useful South," 38. See also Sheldon Hackney, "The South as a Counterculture," *American Scholar* 42 (Spring 1973): 283–93, and C. Vann Woodward, "The Southern Ethic in a Puritan World," *William and Mary Quarterly* 25 (July 1968): 343–70.

9. Choong Soon Kim, *An Asian Anthropologist in the South: Field Experiences with Blacks, Indians, and Whites* (Knoxville: University of Tennessee Press, 1977), 131.

10. King, *Southern Ladies and Gentlemen*, 228–29.

11. Laura Richardson, "Breaking Ranks with Reality," *Texas Observer*, 25 April 1980, 8. The article actually deals with Norman Podhoretz's strictures on Southern writers. Podhoretz, Richardson notes, assumes "that good manners are *sinister*. They are, in his opinion, a hypocritical ruse designed to conceal our voracious lust for advancement." (This from the author of *Making It!*)

12. Linda K. Lanier, "Yankees in Dixie: Cultures in Collision," *U.S. News & World Report*, 7 March 1983, 56.

13. Quoted in "Southern Belles vs. the Yanks," *Tampa Tribune*, 23 December 1984, 9-I.

14. Roy Reed, "Revisiting the Southern Mind," *New York Times Magazine*, 5 December 1976, 99.

15. Eudora Welty, *The Ponder Heart* (New York: Harcourt, Brace & World, 1954), 11.

16. Frady, "Skirmishes," 216 (emphasis added).

17. Roy Blount, Jr., *What Men Don't Tell Women* (New York: Penguin Books, 1984), 26.

18. Frady, "Skirmishes," 218.

19. Ibid., 219–20.

20. Quoted in "Southern Belles vs. the Yanks," 1-I.

21. King, *Southern Ladies and Gentlemen*, 58.

22. Tom Wolfe, *Radical Chic & Mau-mauing the Flak Catchers* (New York: Farrar, Straus and Giroux, 1970), 32–33, 40–42.

23. Will Herberg, *Protestant—Catholic—Jew: An Essay in American Religious Sociology* (Garden City, New York: Doubleday, 1956), 41–45. Herberg quotes Marcus Hansen on "the principle of third-generation interest": "what the son wishes to forget, the grandson wishes to remember."

24. Reed, "Revisiting the Southern Mind," 99.

25. Roebuck and Hickson, *The Southern Redneck*, 69, 170–72.

26. "Those Good Ole Boys," 47. It may be that the middle classes appropriated the

label sometime during the seventies. If so, it would explain the late 1970s rehabilitation of the term "redneck": it was all the working class was left with. (For examples of a very positive image, indistinguishable from that of the working-class good old boy, see AuCoin, *Redneck*, and "Redneck Chic!" *Friday Extra!* [supplement to *Tampa Tribune*], 23 May 1980.) At the same time, "redneck" in its pejorative sense has been applied to middle-class good old boys by those who dislike them. Will Campbell ("The World of the Redneck," 37–38) distinguishes between his "honest-to-God poverty-stricken brothers and sisters in the boondocks and hollers" and "the middle-class redneck" (so-called by "sophisticates") who may be simply "the guy who drives a Grand Prix with lots of chrome to the country club."

27. Frady, "Skirmishes," 218. The first Mrs. Wallace was "a quiet, singularly uncomplicated but altogether pleasant woman whom [George] had found behind the counter of a dime store" (216, 218). The second was, by some accounts, a good old girl.

28. Ken Emerson, "Country Music—Confusion in Profusion," *New York Times*, 18 November 1979, 31D. Emerson nevertheless liked the album for its high spirits. He also recommended Willie Nelson's version of "Santa Claus Is Coming to Town."

29. Anne Roiphe, "The Waltons: Ma and Pa and John-Boy in Mythic America," *New York Times Magazine*, 18 November 1973, 132. The same article juxtaposed stills from the series with Walker Evans photographs, with the naive caption: "The Depression—real and recreated."

30. Inge K. Broverman, Susan Raymond Vogel, Donald M. Broverman, Frank E. Clarkson, and Paul S. Rosenkrantz, "Sex-Role Stereotypes: A Current Appraisal," *Journal of Social Issues* 28, no. 2 (1972): 63. The literature on sex roles and sex-role stereotypes is now vast; Broverman et al. offer a review, now largely out-of-date. For a somewhat more recent summary, see Richard D. Ashmore and Frances K. Del Boca, "Sex Stereotypes and Implicit Personality Theory: Toward a Cognitive–Social Psychological Conceptualization," *Sex Roles* 5 (February 1979): 219–48.

31. John C. Athanassiades, "The Internalization of the Female Stereotype by College Women," *Human Relations* 30 (February 1977): 187–99, reports that college women's self-reported "public selves" often conformed more closely to their "perceptions of the female stereotype" than did their self-images. (No doubt the same was often true for Sambo; see above, p. 7.) Following social psychologists' custom, Athanassiades reported his findings as if they came

from beyond time and place, but since he was reporting from Georgia State University, his findings may be particularly valuable in the present context.

32. Percy, *Lancelot*, 128.
33. Chappell, "The South in Film," 310.
34. Blount, "Two-Dollar Dogs," 4–5.
35. Kirby, "The Southern 'Catch 22,'" 12. A reformed New Yorker, Verschuure, is also indignant in "Stumble, Bumble, Mumble." He means well, but I find his argument undermined by his belief that there is a "true Southern experience," and that "The Waltons" presents it.
36. Blount, *What Men Don't Tell Women*, 28–29.

Works Cited

Addis, Don. "Real Men Don't Eat Kwitchy." *The Floridian* (supplement to *St. Petersburg Times*), 11 July 1982, 5.

Agee, James, and Walker Evans. *Let Us Now Praise Famous Men*. Boston: Houghton Mifflin, 1941.

Allen, Irving Lewis. *The Language of Ethnic Conflict: Social Organization and Lexical Culture*. New York: Columbia University Press, 1983.

Ashmore, Richard D., and Frances K. Del Boca. "Sex Stereotypes and Implicit Personality Theory: Toward a Cognitive–Social Psychological Conceptualization." *Sex Roles* 5 (February 1979): 219–48.

Athanassiades, John C. "The Internalization of the Female Stereotype by College Women." *Human Relations* 30 (February 1977): 187–99.

AuCoin, Bill. *Redneck*. Matteson, Ill.: Greatlakes Living Press, 1977.

Baldwin, Joseph G. *The Flush Times of Alabama and Mississippi*. 1853; reprint ed., Gloucester, Mass.: Peter Smith, 1974.

Banes, Ruth A. "Continuity and Change in the Myth of the Southern Woman: Country Women and Rhinestone Cowgirls." Paper presented at conference on Southern women, Georgia State University, 6 March 1981.

_____. "Mythology in Music: The Ballad of Loretta Lynn." *Canadian Review of American Studies*, in press.

_____. "Southern Women in Country Songs." *Journal of Regional Cultures* 1 (Fall–Winter 1982): 57–70.

Bargainnier, Earl F. "Tin Pan Alley and Dixie: The South in Popular Song." *Mississippi Quarterly* 30 (Fall 1977): 527–64.

Becker, Howard. *Outsiders: Studies in the Sociology of Deviance*. Glencoe, Ill.: Free Press, 1963.

Bell, Quentin. *On Human Finery*, rev. ed. New York: Schocken Books, 1976.

Bertelson, David. *The Lazy South*. New York: Oxford University Press, 1967.

Black, Merle, and John Shelton Reed. "Blacks and Southerners: A Research Note." *Journal of Politics* 44 (February 1982): 165–71.

Blount, Roy, Jr. "C'mon, They're Not All Dumber than Two-Dollar Dogs." *TV Guide*, 2 February 1980, 4–8.

———. *Crackers: This Whole Many-Angled Thing of Jimmy, More Carters, Ominous Little Animals, Sad-Singing Women, My Daddy and Me.* New York: Alfred A. Knopf, 1980.

———. *What Men Don't Tell Women.* New York: Penguin Books, 1984.

Boney, F. N. "The American South." *Journal of Popular Culture* 10 (Summer 1976): 293.

———. "The Redneck." *Georgia Review* 25 (Fall 1971): 333–42.

———. "The Southern Aristocrat." *Midwest Quarterly* 15 (Spring 1974): 215–30.

———. *Southerners All.* Macon: Mercer University Press, 1984.

Boorstin, Daniel J. *The Image; or, What Happened to the American Dream.* New York: Atheneum, 1962.

Branscome, James. "Annihilating the Hillbilly: The Appalachians' Struggle with America's Institutions." *Katallagete* 3 (Winter 1971): 25–32.

Briggs, Joe Bob. "Joe Bob issues a Communist Alert for Massillon." *Cleveland Plain Dealer*, 29 March 1985, 12.

Broverman, Inge K., Susan Raymond Vogel, Donald M. Broverman, Frank E. Clarkson, and Paul S. Rosenkrantz. "Sex-Role Stereotypes: A Current Appraisal." *Journal of Social Issues* 28, no. 2 (1972): 59–78.

Bufwack, Mary. "The Feminist Sensibility in Post-War Country Music." *Southern Quarterly* 12 (Spring 1984): 135–44.

Caldwell, Erskine, and Margaret Bourke-White. *You Have Seen Their Faces.* New York: Modern Age Books, 1937.

Campbell, Edward D. C., Jr. *The Celluloid South: The Old South in American Film, 1903–1978.* Knoxville: University of Tennessee Press, 1981.

Campbell, Will D. "The World of the Redneck." *Katallagete* 5 (Spring 1974): 34–40.

Cash, W. J. *The Mind of the South.* New York: Alfred A. Knopf, 1941.

Chandler, C. R., and H. Paul Chalfant. "The Sexual Double Standard in Country Music Song Lyrics." *Free Inquiry in Creative Sociology* 13 (November 1985), 155–59.

Chandler, C. R., H. Paul Chalfant, and Craig P. Chalfant. "Cheaters Sometimes Win: Sexual Infidelity in Country Music." In *Forbidden Fruits: Taboos and Tabooism in Culture*, edited by Ray B. Browne. Bowling Green, Ohio: Bowling Green University Popular Press, 1984.

Chappell, Fred. "The Image of the South in Film." *Southern Humanities Review* 12 (Fall 1978): 303–11.

"Cheatin' Men & Sufferin' Women." *Woman's Day,* 4 November 1980, 22–23.

Cobb, James C. "From Muskogee to Luckenbach: Country Music and the 'Southernization' of America." *Journal of Popular Culture* 16 (Winter 1982): 81–91.

Coffin, Tristram Potter. *The Female Hero in Folklore and Legend.* New York: Seabury Press, 1975.

Colvert, James B. "Views of Southern Character in Some Northern Novels." *Mississippi Quarterly* 18 (Spring 1965): 59–68.

Connelly, Thomas L. *The Marble Man: Robert E. Lee and His Image in American Society.* New York: Alfred A. Knopf, 1977.

Connelly, Thomas L., and Barbara L. Bellows. *God and General Longstreet: The Lost Cause and the Southern Mind.* Baton Rouge: Louisiana State University Press, 1982.

Cook, Sylvia Jenkins. *From Tobacco Road to Route 66: The Southern Poor White in Fiction.* Chapel Hill: University of North Carolina Press, 1976.

Core, George. "The Literary Marketplace and the Southern Writer Today." *Southern Review* 21 (April 1985): 306–7.

Crider, Bill. "Sons of *Tobacco Road:* 'Backwoods' Novels." *Journal of Popular Culture* 16 (Winter 1982): 47–59.

Denisoff, R. Serge, and Richard A. Peterson, eds. *The Sounds of Social Change.* Chicago: Rand McNally, 1972.

Egerton, John, and Frye Gaillard. "The Mountaineer Minority." *Race Relations Reporter,* March 1974, 8–13.

Elkins, Stanley. *Slavery: A Problem in American Institutional and Intellectual Life,* 3d ed. Chicago: University of Chicago Press, 1976.

Emerson, Ken. "Country Music—Confusion in Profusion." *New York Times,* 18 November 1979, 31D.

Faulkner, William. *Absalom, Absalom!* New York: Random House, 1936.

Floan, Howard R. *The South in Northern Eyes, 1831 to 1861.* New York: McGraw-Hill, 1958.

Flynt, Wayne. *Dixie's Forgotten People: The South's Poor Whites.* Bloomington: Indiana University Press, 1979.

Frady, Marshall. "Skirmishes with the Ladies of the Magnolias." *Playboy,* September 1972, 121, 214–22.

———. *Wallace.* New York: New American Library, 1975.

Frazier, E. Franklin. "Certain Aspects of Conflict in the Negro Family." *Social Forces* 10 (October 1931): 76–84.

French, Warren, ed. *The South and Film*. Jackson: University Press of Mississippi, 1981.

Freund, Julien. *The Sociology of Max Weber*. New York: Vintage Books, 1969.

Gaines, Francis Pendleton. *The Southern Plantation: A Study in the Development and the Accuracy of a Tradition*. New York: Columbia University Press, 1925.

Gerster, Patrick, and Nicholas Cords, eds. *Myth and Southern History*, 2 vols. Chicago: Rand McNally, 1974.

Godwin, Gail. "The Southern Belle." *Ms.*, July 1975, 49–52, 84–85.

Goldstein, Richard. "My Country Music Problem—and Yours." *Mademoiselle*, June 1973, 114–15, 185.

Green, Archie. "Hillbilly Music: Source and Symbol." *Journal of American Folklore* 78 (July–September 1965): 204–26.

Green, Lewis. *How Tuh Live in the Kooky South Without Eatin' Grits: A Fun Guide Book fer Yankees*. Highlands, N.C.: The Merry Mountaineers, 1978.

Greene, Johnny. "The Dixie Smile." *Harper's*, September 1976, 14–19.

Gritzner, Charles F. "Country Music: A Reflection of Popular Culture." *Journal of Popular Culture* 11 (Spring 1978): 857–64.

Hackney, Sheldon. "The South as a Counterculture." *American Scholar* 42 (Spring 1973): 283–93.

Hagler, D. Harland. "The Ideal Woman in the Antebellum South: Lady or Farmwife?" *Journal of Southern History* 46 (August 1980): 405–18.

Hawley, Fred. "The Black Legend in Southern Studies." Paper presented to the annual meeting of the Mid-South Sociological Association, Jackson, Mississippi, 1982.

Herberg, Will. *Protestant—Catholic—Jew: An Essay in American Religious Sociology*. Garden City, New York: Doubleday, 1956.

Hicks, Michael. *The South Made Simple*. Austin: Texas Monthly Press, 1982.

Hobson, Fred. *Tell About the South: The Southern Rage to Explain*. Baton Rouge: Louisiana State University Press, 1983.

Hundley, Daniel R. *Social Relations in Our Southern States*. 1860; reprint ed., Baton Rouge: Louisiana State University Press, 1979.

Jackman, Mary R., and Robert W. Jackman. *Class Awareness in the United States*. Berkeley: University of California Press, 1983.

Kaplan, Burton. *Blue Ridge: An Appalachian Community in Transition*. Morgantown: Appalachian Center, West Virginia University, 1971.

Killian, Lewis. *White Southerners*. New York: Random House, 1970.

Kim, Choong Soon. *An Asian Anthropologist in the South: Field Experiences with Blacks, Indians, and Whites*. Knoxville: University of Tennessee Press, 1977.

King, Florence. *Confessions of a Failed Southern Lady.* New York: St. Martin's/Marek, 1985.

———. "The Good Ole Boy." *Harper's,* May 1974, 78–82.

———. "Red Necks, White Socks, and Blue Ribbon Fear." *Harper's,* July 1974, 30–34.

———. *Southern Ladies and Gentlemen.* New York: Bantam Books, 1976.

King, Larry L. "We Ain't Trash No More." *Esquire,* November 1976, 88–90, 152–56.

Kirby, Jack Temple. *Media-Made Dixie: The South in the American Imagination.* Baton Rouge: Louisiana State University Press, 1978.

———. "The Southern 'Catch 22.'" *Southern Partisan,* Fall 1981, 10–12.

Klapp, Orrin E. *Heroes, Villains, and Fools: The Changing American Character.* Englewood Cliffs, N.J.: Prentice-Hall, 1962.

Koon, George William. "Tammy Wynette and the Objective Correlative." *Studies in Popular Culture* 6 (1983): 47–52.

Lanier, Linda K. "Yankees in Dixie: Cultures in Collision." *U.S. News & World Report,* 7 March 1983, 55–56.

Latham, Aaron. "The Ballad of the Urban Cowboy: America's Search for True Grit." *Esquire,* 12 September 1978, 21–30.

Lyle, Katie Letcher. "Southern Country Music: A Brief Eulogy." In *The American South: Portrait of a Culture,* edited by Louis D. Rubin, Jr. Baton Rouge: Louisiana State University Press, 1980.

Manuel, Athan, J. S. Reed, and Charles R. Wilson. "*Playboy's* Southern Exposure." In *Perspectives on the American South: An Annual Review of Politics, Culture, and Society,* vol. 4, edited by James Cobb and Charles R. Wilson. New York: Gordon & Breach, Science Publishers, in press.

Marcus, Greil. *Mystery Train: Images of America in Rock 'n' Roll Music.* New York: E. P. Dutton, 1975.

McGee, Marsha G. "Prime-Time Dixie: Television's View of a 'Simple' South." *Journal of American Culture* 6 (Fall 1983): 100–109.

McIlwaine, Shields. *The Southern Poor-White from Lubberland to Tobacco Road.* 1939; reprint ed., New York: Cooper Square Publishers, 1970.

McKern, Sharon. *Redneck Mothers, Good Ol' Girls and Other Southern Belles: A Celebration of the Women of Dixie.* New York: Viking Press, 1979.

Mencken, H. L. "The Sahara of Bozart." In *American Essays,* edited by Charles B. Shaw. New York: Pelican Mentor Books, 1948.

Merton, Robert K. "Insiders and Outsiders: A Chapter in the Sociology of Knowledge." *American Journal of Sociology* 78 (July 1972): 9–47.

_____. *Social Theory and Social Structure*, rev. ed. Glencoe, Ill.: Free Press, 1957.

Miller, William Lee. *Yankee from Georgia: The Emergence of Jimmy Carter*. New York: Time Books, 1978.

Newcomb, Horace. "Appalachia on Television: Region as Symbol in American Popular Culture." *Appalachian Journal* 7 (Autumn–Winter 1979–80): 155–64.

Norden, Helen Brown. *The Hussy's Handbook*, rev. ed. New York: Arden, 1944.

Nunnally, Pat. "The South Created: Image Making in the National Press." Unpublished paper, Vanderbilt University, 1980.

Odum, Howard W. *The Way of the South: Toward the Regional Balance of America*. New York: Macmillan, 1947, 197–207.

Oerman, Robert K. "Mother, Sister, Sweetheart, Pal: Women in Old-Time Country Music." *Southern Quarterly* 12 (Spring 1984): 125–34.

Osgood, Charles E., George J. Suci, and Percy H. Tannenbaum. *The Measurement of Meaning*. Urbana: University of Illinois Press, 1957.

Owsley, Frank Lawrence. *Plain Folk of the Old South*. Baton Rouge: Louisiana State University Press, 1949.

Parmley, Ingram. "Stalking the Good Old Boy." In *Perspectives on the American South*, vol. 1, edited by Merle Black and J. S. Reed. New York: Gordon & Breach, Science Publishers, 1981.

Patrick, Ralph C., Jr. "A Cultural Approach to Stratification." Ph.D. diss., Harvard University, 1953.

Percy, Walker. *Lancelot*. New York: Avon Books, 1977.

_____. "Questions They Never Asked Me." *Esquire*, December 1977, 170–72, 184–94.

Pettigrew, Thomas F. "Complexity and Change in American Racial Patterns: A Social Psychological View." In *The Negro American*, edited by Talcott Parsons and Kenneth B. Clark. Boston: Beacon Press, 1967.

Pierce, Robert M. "Jimmy Carter and the New South: The View from New York." In *Perspectives on the American South: An Annual Review of Politics, Culture, and Society*, vol. 2, edited by Merle Black and J. S. Reed. New York: Gordon & Breach, Science Publishers, 1984.

Pyron, Darden A. *Recasting: "Gone with the Wind" in American Culture*. Gainesville: University Presses of Florida, 1983.

"Redneck Chic!" *Friday Extra!* (supplement to *Tampa Tribune*), 23 May 1980.

Reed, John Shelton. *The Enduring South: Subcultural Persistence in Mass Society*. Lexington, Mass.: D. C. Heath, 1972.

_____. "Getting to Know You: The 'Contact Hypothesis' Applied to the Sectional

Beliefs and Attitudes of White Southerners." *Social Forces* 59 (September 1980): 123–35.

———. "Life and Leisure in the New South." *North Carolina Historical Review* 60 (April 1983): 172–82.

———. *One South: An Ethnic Approach to Regional Culture.* Baton Rouge: Louisiana State University Press, 1982.

———. "The *Prevailing* South?" *National Humanities Center Newsletter* 5, no. 4 (Summer 1984): 1–7.

———. *Southerners: The Social Psychology of Sectionalism.* Chapel Hill: University of North Carolina Press, 1983.

Reed, Roy. "Revisiting the Southern Mind." *New York Times Magazine,* 5 December 1976, 42–43, 99–108.

Richardson, Laura. "Breaking Ranks with Reality." *Texas Observer,* 25 April 1980, 6–9, 18–19.

Rifkin, Jeremy, and Ted Howard. *Redneck Power: The Wit and Wisdom of Billy Carter.* New York: Bantam Books, 1977.

Rodgers, Raymond S. "Images of Rednecks in Country Music: The Lyrical Persona of a Southern Superman." *Journal of Regional Cultures* 1 (Fall–Winter 1981): 71–81.

Roebuck, Julian B., and Mark Hickson III. *The Southern Redneck: A Phenomenological Case Study.* New York: Praeger Publishers, 1982.

Roebuck, Julian B., and Ronald L. Neff. "The Multiple Reality of the 'Redneck': Toward a Grounded Theory of the Southern Class Structure." *Studies in Symbolic Interaction* 3 (1980): 233–62.

Rogers, Gayle J. "The Changing Image of the Southern Woman: A Performer on a Pedestal." *Journal of Popular Culture* 16 (Winter 1982): 60–67.

Rogers, Jimmie N. *The Country Music Message: All About Lovin' and Livin'.* Englewood Cliffs, N.J.: Prentice-Hall, 1983.

Rogers, Tommy W. "D. R. Hundley: A Multi-Class Thesis of Social Stratification in the Antebellum South." *Mississippi Quarterly* 23 (Spring 1970): 135–54.

———. "Daniel R. Hundley's Contribution to Folklore." *Alabama Historical Quarterly* 30 (Fall–Winter 1968): 203–18.

Roiphe, Anne. "The Waltons: Ma and Pa and John-Boy in Mythic America." *New York Times Magazine,* 18 November 1973, 40–41, 130–34, 146.

Rubin, Louis D., Jr. *The Wary Fugitives: Four Poets and the South.* Baton Rouge: Louisiana State University Press, 1978.

Sale, Kirkpatrick. *Power Shift: The Rise of the Southern Rim and Its Challenge to the Eastern Establishment.* New York: Vintage Books, 1976.

Satchell, Michael. "Jimmy's Brother Billy: 'I'm a Real Southern Boy.'" Raleigh *News and Observer,* 15 November 1976, 1, 6.

Scheff, Thomas J. *Being Mentally Ill: A Sociological Theory.* Chicago: Aldine, 1966.

Scott, Anne Firor. *The Southern Lady: From Pedestal to Politics, 1830–1930.* Chicago: University of Chicago Press, 1970.

Shapiro, Henry D. *Appalachia on Our Mind: The Southern Mountains and Mountaineers in the American Consciousness, 1870–1920.* Chapel Hill: University of North Carolina Press, 1978.

Sherrill, Robert. *Gothic Politics in the Deep South: Stars of the New Confederacy.* New York: Ballantine Books, 1969.

––––––. "The Pork Chop Conspiracy." *New York Times Magazine,* 10 October 1976, 111.

Sims, Barbara B. "'She's Got to be a Saint, Lord Knows I Ain't': Feminine Masochism in American Country Music." *Journal of Country Music* 5 (Spring 1974): 24–30.

Skaggs, Merrill Maguire. *The Folk of Southern Fiction.* Athens: University of Georgia Press, 1972.

Smith, Stephen A. *Myth, Media, and the Southern Mind.* Fayetteville: University of Arkansas Press, 1985.

––––––. "The Old South Myth as a Contemporary Southern Commodity." *Journal of Popular Culture* 16 (Winter 1982): 22–29.

Soderbergh, Peter A. "Hollywood and the South, 1930–1960." *Mississippi Quarterly* 19 (Winter 1965–1966): 1–19.

––––––. "The South in Juvenile Series Books, 1907–1917." *Mississippi Quarterly* 27 (Spring 1974): 131–40.

"Southern Belles vs. the Yanks." *Tampa Tribune,* 23 December 1984, 1-I, 9-I.

"'Terrible Ted': Turner's Bid for CBS Viewed as Outlandish, Fits In With His Image." *Wall Street Journal,* 19 April 1985, 1, 6.

Thompson, Edgar T. "Decency and the Good Old Boy Syndrome." *South Atlantic Quarterly* 83 (Autumn 1984): 434–46.

"Those Good Ole Boys." *Time,* 27 September 1976, 47.

Tindall, George Brown. *The Ethnic Southerners.* Baton Rouge: Louisiana State University Press, 1976.

––––––. "Sunbelt Snow Job." *Houston Review* 1 (Spring 1979): 3–13.

Vander Mey, Brenda J. "Southern Women and Country Music: Myths, Messages, and Contradictory Imagery." Unpublished paper, Department of Sociology, Clemson University, n.d.

Vander Mey, Brenda J., and Ellen S. Bryant. "Southern Sex Roles: Country Music as the Vehicle for Investigation." Paper presented at meeting of the Southern Sociological Society, Atlanta, April 1983.

Vanover, J. R. "The Useful South." *Southern Partisan,* April 1980, 38.

Verschuure, Eric Peter. "Stumble, Bumble, Mumble: TV's Image of the South." *Journal of Popular Culture* 16 (Winter 1982): 92–96.

Wallerstein, Immanuel. *The Capitalist World-Economy.* Cambridge: Cambridge University Press, 1979.

Weaver, Blanche H. C. "D. R. Hundley: Subjective Sociologist." *Georgia Review* 10 (Summer 1956): 222–34.

Weber, Max. "Class, Status, Party." In *From Max Weber: Essays in Sociology,* edited by H. H. Gerth and C. Wright Mills. New York: Oxford University Press, 1958.

Welty, Eudora. *The Ponder Heart.* New York: Harcourt, Brace & World, 1954.

Whisnant, David E. "Ethnicity and the Recovery of Regional Identity in Appalachia: Thoughts upon Entering the Zone of Occult Instability." *Soundings: An Interdisciplinary Journal* 56 (Spring 1973): 124–38.

Wilgus, D. K. "Country-Western Music and the Urban Hillbilly." *Journal of American Folklore* 83 (April–June 1970): 175–79.

Wilson, Charles R. *Baptized in Blood: The Religion of the Lost Cause, 1865–1920.* Athens: University of Georgia Press, 1980.

Wilson, Edmund. *Patriotic Gore: Studies in the Literature of the American Civil War.* New York: Oxford University Press, 1966.

Wolfe, Margaret Ripley. "The Southern Lady: Long Suffering Counterpart of the Good Ole Boy." *Journal of Popular Culture* 11 (Summer 1977): 18–27.

Wolfe, Tom. *The Kandy-Kolored Tangerine-Flake Streamline Baby.* New York: Pocket Books, 1966.

———. *Radical Chic & Mau-mauing the Flak Catchers.* New York: Farrar, Straus and Giroux, 1970.

Woodward, C. Vann. "The Southern Ethic in a Puritan World." *William and Mary Quarterly* 25 (July 1968): 343–70.

———. "Southern Styles, Black and White." *Chapel Hill Weekly,* 16 April 1972, Section II, 1, 4.

Wyatt-Brown, Bertram. *Southern Honor: Ethics and Behavior in the Old South.* New York: Oxford University Press, 1982.

Yoder, Edwin M., Jr. *The Night of the Old South Ball, and Other Essays and Fables.* Oxford, Miss.: Yoknapatawpha Press, 1984.

Index